WWII—Army Air Force Chronicles

WWII—Army Air Force Chronicles

Jerome ("J.R.") Roth

VANTAGE PRESS
New York

Cover design by Polly McQuillen

FIRST EDITION

Published by Vantage Press, Inc.
419 Park Ave. South, New York, NY 10016

Manufactured in the United States of America
ISBN: 978-0-533-15880-5

Library of Congress Catalog Card No.: 2007933756

0 9 8 7 6 5 4 3 2 1

To Gussie Roth

Contents

Author's Note

This is a story about a teenage boy at the start of and during World War II. This young boy realized that America would soon be in the war that was raging in Europe and that he was draft age. He knew that if he were drafted he would be assigned to the infantry. He knew that was not for him. He wanted to be in the Army Air Corps.

WWII—Army Air Force Chronicles

I
Prologue

It all started when two families, one living in Billarus, Russia and the other living in Vienna, Austria, decided to go to America at the end of 1800s. This was a period when discrimination and anti-Semitism was raging in Europe. Both families settled in New York City and they both brought with them infants. The Russian family, a baby girl and the Austrian family, a baby boy. Both grew up and attended the public school system of New York City.

Gussie, the girl, after public school, instead of going to the high school, decided to go to commercial school, which was part of the public school system. She learned bookkeeping, typing and office skills.

Time marched on and now the two children were grown up and out of school. Gussie had to take care of her two stepbrothers who were born after her father died and her mother remarried. After the two children were old enough to go to school, she got a job as a bookkeeper in a brass factory. The boy, now a man, eventually started to manufacture ladies dresses. This was the period when unions were starting to organize small businesses; the union organization was composed of roughnecks and gangsters. They organized Morris' factory by intimidating the seamstresses by waiting for them to leave work at night and wait for them on or around the corner and accosted them, warning them of the consequences if they refused to sign up. After the factory was unionized, the union delegate came into the factory once a week, and without a word, went straight to the register and removed the workers' dues.

Gussie was not pleased with the atmosphere of the brass factory; in addition, the owner kept a gun in the desk drawer. After a year or so, she decided to leave the job and assist her stepfather Joe in his tie factory where she not only kept the books but in the more technical aspect of the job, she dealt with the factors who lent money to small manufacturers. She had to show them the company books in order to assure them that they could repay the loan. While her stepfather was on the road selling to haberdashers and department stores, she ran the factory.

On a trip to Kansas City, Missouri, Joe visited Harry Truman Men's Clothing Store, the same Harry Truman that later became the President of the United States. Mr. Truman was in the back room playing cards with his political friends. It seemed Mr. Truman was a customer of Joe's and owed him for an order of ties that he had purchased. Mr. Truman told Joe that business was bad and he couldn't pay for the ties. Joe told Mr. Truman that if he spent more time with his business and less time playing cards, he would be able to pay his debts. Mr. Truman eventually went bankrupt and Joe never collected Mr. Truman's debt.

One day Gussie's friend Agnes introduced her to Morris, a handsome young man with a very bright future. In time, Morris proposed and Gussie accepted. Of course, she asked her parents for permission; this was a very hard pill for her stepfather to swallow, since it was Gussie that helped her mother with the housework and ran the factory with no pay. Her stepfather objected, but in spite of the objection, Gussie married Morris and they bought a two-family house in Bensonhurst, Brooklyn. As time went by, Gussie and Morris had two boys.

When the boys were ages three and six years old, a terrible flu epidemic was sweeping across the country and Morris became very ill. There was little the doctors could do since this was the mid-1920s and there were no antibiotics at that time. And tragically, Morris died and Gussie became ill herself and was taken to the hospital. While Gussie was in the hospital, Melvin, the older son, became ill. Fearing the ailment that was raging, they made every effort to keep the two boys apart. Fortunately, Gussie and Melvin recovered.

Gussie was now alone with two very young boys to care for with no economic support. All Gussie could think of was returning to her parents who were now living in Kansas City, Missouri.

The trip was long and difficult with two active little boys. Joe still held a grudge against Gussie and her mother was very concerned about the children soiling the living room furniture. There were severe restrictions placed on the children and after a number of months, Gussie packed up and went back to Brooklyn. She sold the two-family house in Bensonhurst, Brooklyn which she shared with her tenants, the Goodman family, who subsequently established the Goodman Noodle Company.

Gussie now had to determine how she would earn her living. She felt that by being a bookkeeper, it would not earn her enough money to raise two children, to have the ability to send them to college, and to live comfortably. She decided to visit a relative who was in the real estate business and was successful in order to learn as much as she could about the business. Another relative was a dentist who asked Gussie if she was interested in participating in a real estate deal. She felt it was a good opportunity and she became a partner, owning a twenty-five percent interest.

Time marched on and along came 1929, the stock market crash and the Great Depression. Sometime in the first part of the 1930s, the owner of the apartment house began losing tenants until he found that he could no longer pay his mortgage payments and had to give up his ownership interest. The medical group, which held the first mortgage, contacted the dentist Dr. Cohen and asked him if he wished to manage the building. Dr. Cohen couldn't given up his dental practice so he called Gussie and explained the situation to her. Since Gussie couldn't afford to lose her investment she told Dr. Cohen that she would run the building.

When Gussie first visited the building she found that she had a big problem on her hands. The apartments were only half full and were in very poor condition. She found renting them was impossible. Her desire to save her investment led her to an idea. She visited the medical group that was holding the first mortgage and asked them to forgo the mortgage payments for a short period of time so she could use the money to purchase a new type of icebox called a refrigerator. Prior to the new invention called the refrigerator everyone had an icebox consisting of two chambers. On the top, there was a chamber holding a large cake of ice and on the bottom was a much larger chamber holding the food. In the 1920s and 1930s, the iceman came in his horse and wagon with large slabs of ice that he chopped down to the icebox size and carried them on his back to his customers. The new gas refrigerator, little by little, put the iceman out of business.

With the new invention of the refrigerator, and with Gussie able to purchase them for the vacant apartments, she was able to rent out some of the apartments. She would place ads in the newspaper and as people came to view the apartments, Gussie was there to show them around and offer them the new refrigerator and that was a very tempting offer. Over a relatively short period most of the apartments were rented and as soon as the income permitted, Gussie went back to the medical group and gave them the good news. She could resume paying interest and amortization. This was, of course, an indicator that a lot of the unemployed were finding jobs and the Depression was easing. Gussie realized that this was a good time to pick up buildings that were losing money and owned by bank institutions and speculators who were anxious to unload a losing investment.

Gussie was aware that her stepfather, the tie manufacturer, was investing in stocks since his business was doing well. She contacted him and proposed an investment in real estate. Joe thought that it was a good idea, if she could find a good proposition. Gussie was off and running. She contacted friends who could help her locate buildings that were good prospects. In a relatively short time she received the addresses of a few buildings. When Gussie decided to visit these buildings, she took her son, J.R., with her. The first building was a six-story elevator building. The building had a crack visible on the side that ran from the bottom to the top. Gussie pointed this out to J.R. stating that this was a poor prospect. The next building backed up to the subway tracks. Gussie kept looking until she found a building which was in a good location and had other good features, such as good apartment layouts and good construction.

During this period of time, her two sons were growing up and progressing throughout the struggle to save her investments and find and recommend buildings for her stepfather to invest in. This meant working from 6 a.m. to 11 p.m. seven days a week. The youngest boy J.R. attended P.S. 189, a notoriously poor school. He was eventually sent to a newly constructed school called Winthrop Junior High.

The first day at Winthrop, all the children were sent to

the auditorium where they were tested to determine how much they learned at P.S. 189. Most of the students were at the fourth grade level. They knew they had to start from grade four and bring them up to the eighth grade before they could start to teach them at the start of Junior High School. This Junior High was run like a parochial school. The students had to wear a white shirt, red tie, and dark pants. They had to walk in the hallway from class in formation two by two and no talking. One day J.R., who loved to talk and kid around, was talking to a friend when a teacher slapped him in the face and told him to keep quiet. It stunned him and was very effective.

One nasty day, J.R. saw a bedraggled dog who managed to gain access to the lobby of the building that J.R. lived in. J.R. liked cats and dogs and wanted to try to make friends with the dog and to get him to follow him upstairs to his apartment. He managed to coax the dog up one flight of stairs, but the dog refused to go any further. J.R. ran and got his mom, who was home at the time. Gussie offered the dog some food, realizing the dog was hungry. The dog ran up the stairs and followed Gussie to the apartment. Gussie put a pillow under the stove and gave the dog some water and a bowl of food. The dog drank and ate and settled contently on the pillow.

Later that day, the dog needed to go out. He walked to the entrance door of the apartment and scratched. J.R. heard this noise but didn't know what it was, so he investigated. When he got to the source of the noise he saw the dog, and realized he needed to go outside. J.R. opened the door and let the dog go out. He didn't know how he got out of the lobby but he did, and after a short period of time, he somehow got back into the lobby and somehow found his way back to the apartment. He then commenced to scratch on the door, but since it was over an hour after J.R. had let the dog out, he did not know what the noise meant. But again, being curious, he got to the source of the noise and opened the door and in trotted the dog, much to the surprise and delight of J.R. The dog was so dirty that Gussie decided he needed a bath, but being unfamiliar with dogs, she did not want to attempt it herself. Gussie, therefore, decided to call the super of the building she managed. He agreed to bathe the dog. The super came over and picked up the dog. The next day, Gussie received a call from the super who asked her if she wanted to keep the dog. After all, the dog is a responsibility. Gussie told him that the kids would be terribly upset if she let him go.

When the super brought the dog back, at that time, it seemed like the dog had transformed. It was incredible. The dog's long hair was silky white with pink skin underneath and brown eyes. He was a beauty. J.R. decided to call him Stranger, Strany for short. Another mouth to be fed, another member of the family.

Meanwhile, the boys progressed through the public school system. One summer when J.R. was about six years old, Gussie received a call from one of her relatives inviting her to come to a small hotel in the Catskill Mountains in upstate New York. In those days a hotel was an old frame one-family house with a large building in the rear that was used for dining and dancing in the evenings. Also in the rear was the lake, which was a very large lake called White Lake. The water was so clear that you could see to the bottom. One sunny day, Gussie decided to take her two boys swimming. She got two rubber tubes for the boys. They had a great time. J.R. swam under the water, examining the bottom and swam out to the deep water with his tube. J.R. suddenly noticed that the air had escaped from the tube. He became very frightened and hurriedly swam back to shore. When he got back to shore, J.R. realized he needed no assistance when in deep water.

One day, J.R. and his brother Melvin, along with a few other boys, swam out to the float and after resting a bit, enjoyed jumping into the water and swimming back to the float. Suddenly Melvin yelled for help. J.R. and all the other boys were in the water and swam to the float and Melvin explained that his toe was impaled by a nail. The gang of kids tried to push the float to shore, but the float was anchored to the bottom. Finally, Melvin was successful in freeing himself. To be on the safe said, Gussie decided to take Melvin to see a doctor in a nearby town. All too quickly the summer vacation was over and the kids were home.

The next summer, Gussie was heavily engaged in managing five buildings and could not be distracted by two very active young boys who were out of school for the summer with nothing but mischief to look forward to. Gussie decided to send the boys to summer camp. When she told the boys of her decisions, although apprehensive, J.R. was interested in the challenge. The camp was located in upstate New York, outside of Port Jervis. The camp had a large man-made lake which was fed by a large mountain stream. They enjoyed the many activities, which included baseball, basketball, swimming, canoeing, rowing and arts and crafts.

Melvin liked basketball and played in a lot of the games. J.R. liked swimming and had his eye on canoeing. In order to go canoeing, you had to pass a very demanding test. J.R. wasn't sure he could pass the test. He felt it was beyond his ability, but he couldn't ignore the temptation. He was required to swim a distance of about 100-plus yards, which was much further than he had ever swam before. With a tremendous effort, he made it. But there was a second part to the test. He had to paddle the canoe out to the deep water and jump out without tipping the canoe over. Then he had to climb into the canoe, which was the hardest part of the test. J.R.'s determination helped him pass the test.

The next summer, J.R. returned to camp, but his brother did not. He had a great time. During the stay, one of the counselors gave a course in junior life saving, which J.R. took and passed. One of the campers told everyone the counselor who gave the course was an FBI man. When asked how he knew, he said he saw his credentials in his wallet he kept in the foot locker. All good things come to an end, and so did camp, although J.R. never forgot it.

Summer was followed by a snowy, icy winter, when the young boys in the area amused themselves by sleigh riding. They had the ideal location for sleighing. They had a park and street that ran alongside of the park, which was on a steep slope. One day, J.R. went out with his sled to enjoy sleighing with his friends, but they were not around. What was he to do? J.R. decided to try the most dangerous slope in the park. It was dangerous not only because it was very steep, but also because it had a lot of trees at the bottom of the slope and the sled had to steer between the trees. Since J.R.'s sled only had one steering arm, it made it even more dangerous. It seemed that Melvin had lent J.R.'s sled to a friend who had broken the steering arm. J.R., however, who was thirteen at the time, did not think of it as dangerous. Instead, he felt it was a challenge.

Down the hill he went and almost immediately he noticed that the slope, which he thought was snowy, was a sheet of ice instead, making it impossible to steer the sled. When he got close to the bottom of the slope, he noticed he was heading straight for a tree. He tried to steer the sled by dragging his left foot to get the sled to go to the right, in order to avoid hitting a tree, but his momentum prevailed and he hit a tree. The sled bounced back and sliced into J.R.'s left leg, cutting the leg near the groin. J.R. lay there in shock. Lucky for J.R., a group of young Italian kids were playing nearby. Seeing J.R. laying there, they ran to investigate.

When they got to J.R., they saw the blood, they picked him up and carried him a few blocks to the end of the park and then out of the park to the street. They flagged down a laundry truck. The driver of the truck took J.R. and put him in the back of the truck with the laundry. He took J.R. to the nearest hospital. J.R. was brought into the emergency room where the doctors worked on him to stop the bleeding. When the doctors were through with emergency procedures, they told everyone in the hospital to go to the emergency room to take a look at the terrible wound. All the doctors, nurses, and interns came in and viewed J.R.'s wound. One of the young doctors was so shocked by what he saw, he shouted at J.R., "Look at what you did!"

J.R. replied, "No way!"

When J.R. was assigned a bed, a doctor came to see him. He introduced himself as the superintendent of the hospital. He told J.R. that he was going to have to operate on him to put "Humpty Dumpty" back together again. The news, of course, frightened J.R. Shortly thereafter, a nurse came into the room and when she started to speak, J.R. realized she was Irish. He asked her if she could do an Irish jig and she obligingly commenced to dance. It was a great diversion.

The next day, J.R. was wheeled into the operating room and he was placed on the operating table. As he lay there, he was very comfortable, until a nurse strapped his legs with a very wide strap. Then two doctors and two nurses held J.R.'s arms and legs and a doctor placed a screen in the shape of a muzzle over his face. The doctor then began to pour ether onto the screen. When J.R. first got a smell of the ether, the battle began. He struggled. First he turned his head away, as close to the table as possible. This made it impossible to hold the screen over his face. When the screen was finally positioned correctly, J.R. turned his face the other way. The doctor finally said, "If he doesn't go under soon, I will."

J.R. finally lost consciousness. He later woke and found himself in bed. The next day, the doctor visited J.R. When he removed the bandages, he found the laceration wide open, which meant the stitches did not hold. The doctor told J.R. that he'd have to put him together again. He then commenced to press the wound together and place the thick straps of tape completely around the thigh. For several days thereafter, he repeated the procedure. Before J.R. was released from the hospital, the doctor told Gussie that he may not be able to stand upright again. When J.R. tried to walk, he was bent over. Gussie did not agree with the doctor. The very next day, she started to take J.R. for walks around the block with his arm around her neck for support. This went on until J.R. was able to stand up straight.

Melvin about this time graduated from Tilden High School. He was the youngest student to go to college. He decided to take up dentistry and entered the New York University premed. After two or three years, he became ill and had to drop out. It was obvious that the teen years had been difficult for the brother. During this time, Gussie was accruing a number of buildings to manage, each of which had many vacancies and a lot of delayed maintenance. The buildings were located in different areas of Brooklyn and therefore needing transportation to manage. Gussie needed a car, but she had never driven a car before. Most of the buildings she managed had coal burning furnaces and coal salesmen were very competitive. Gussie asked one of the salesmen that she purchased coal from to help her learn to drive. Then there was the problem of purchasing a car. That wasn't the only problem.

Gussie sat in the driver's seat and she couldn't reach the gas or brake pedals and couldn't see over the dashboard. At that time, the auto manufacturers built the cars for the average person, who weren't necessarily tall or short. The auto dealers had to add extensions to the gas and brake pedals and raise the driver's seats. This continued to be a problem for years to come.

When J.R. graduated from Winthrop Junior High and was about to start high school his mother decided it was time to leave Crown Heights. She selected an apartment in one of her buildings in Sheepshead Bay. The apartment had two bedrooms, which was an improvement over the one bedroom apartment. In addition it had a very large foyer that led from the entrance to all the rooms in the apartment. Not only were the individual rooms much larger than the last apartment but the foyer was ideal for use as an office. Gussie immediately set out to shop for furniture. Of course she took J.R. with her. Whenever she had to go to court or to a contract signing or to any other important occasion she took J.R. with her.

In addition to caring for two active boys and managing buildings there were additional problems. Since Gussie's stepfather was buying the buildings he insisted the books be kept in Kansas City where he lived and that all checks were signed by him. Just imagine running a business when you had to pay bills by making out a check and first sending it out to Kansas City and waiting for it to be signed and returned before you send it out. In addition not having the books to refer to.

J.R. at this time entered Madison High School with a great incentive to succeed since he lost one term in P.S. 189 due to his sledding accident. He had to walk a mile with a load of books and lunch. When he returned home he had to do his homework and walk the dog. It wasn't all dull; J.R. made a few friends. One of his friends was Joe who introduced him to Arthur who was short in stature but very intelligent. Arthur had a very beautiful sister called Moana who made life interesting for a teenager. During this period, his mother was engaged in her real estate management business. The office being in the apartment it was impossible for J.R. to ignore. He got involved in many different ways. He answered the phone, he talked with supers, contractors, etc. He was learning about the practical side of real estate management without realizing it. One day a dentist friend of the family who was responsible for Gussie's entrance into the real estate business called. It seems he owned a walk-up apartment house (four-story) that was being managed by a relative who was a lawyer. The building was losing money and was in poor shape. The bank that had the mortgage told the dentist to obtain good management or they will foreclose. The dentist asked Gussie if she would be willing to manage the building. Gussie agreed and went over to inspect the building. After inspecting the building she was sorry she agreed to manage it. She was shocked at the condition of the building. One of the apartments on the top floor had no fixtures in the bathroom or the kitchen. Gussie went to work and corrected all the deficiencies and rented all the vacant apartments.

J.R. In his last year at Madison High School decided to try his hand at sports. Since the only sport he did well was swimming, he tried out for the swim team and made it. He enjoyed the competition and the comradeship. He also enjoyed traveling to the different high schools to compete in swim meets. When they visited Brooklyn Technical High School the team availed themselves to a nearby burlesque theater for recreation.

When J.R. joined the swim team the coach asked him what stroke he did best. J.R. said the breaststroke. The coach was delighted since he only had one breaststroker. Before the season started the team had to work out every day in order to get into shape. The regimen was grueling. The first meet was at Lincoln High School. J.R. was to be the second breaststroke swimmer for James Madison High. J.R. was very excited it was to be his first test of his skill. Lincoln High had a relatively new pool which was very large with a balcony which could hold a large number of students to cheer their school alma mater to victory.

J.R. took his place at the starting point along with his teammate and the two swimmers from Lincoln High. The whistle blew and they were off. They had to swim three laps. In the first lap, all four were very closely aligned; in the next lap, J.R.'s teammate took the lead with J.R. and the others close behind. When the four swimmers turned for the third and last lap Madison's lead breaststroker was well in the lead. Lincoln's swimmers were close behind J.R. who was third. The crowd was screaming and J.R. was trying as hard as he could, but as he started the third lap his strength gave out. He slowed precipitously. The Lincoln swimmer who was behind J.R. started to catch up and pass him as the crowd was yelling. J.R. finished last but was awarded third place because the Lincoln swimmer fouled out.

When practice commenced a few days after the meet the coach asked J.R. to swim 100 laps of the pool with the other breaststroker. When J.R. completed the 100 laps he was told that he would be swimming in the medley where they swim two laps. The medley consists of one backstroke swimmer, one breaststroke swimmer and one crawl swimmer. From then on they won every medley contest and held the best time ever in P.S.A.L. that season, until they swam against Erasmus High School. Erasmus placed their best swimmers on their medley team and broke Madison's Record. The Erasmus team was the best swimming team in P.S.A.L. at that time. Finally J.R.'s senior year term ended and J.R. graduated. He was presented with a large M to be sewn on the back of a sweater jacket. He proudly wore his sweater every day thereafter.

Upon graduation from high school J.R. had to decide what he would like to do for a living. J.R. was told to bring his mother to a meeting with a grade advisor as all graduates had to do. The grade advisor who had J.R.'s academic record told his mother that he could choose any profession, doctor, lawyer, engineer or any of the others. J.R. thought about it and decided that since he was exposed to real estate most of his life he should choose real estate.

Now there were decisions to be made, what college and how to finance it. Although J.R. received acceptances from several colleges he chose N.Y.U. In addition he chose to take five courses at night in spite of advice to the contrary. This decision turned out to be a mistake. His marks turned out to be very poor. He took the course every night Monday to Friday. On Friday he took bookkeeping which he slept through every night. One night the teacher woke J.R. He told J.R. that he didn't mind if he slept through his class but objected to the snoring.

J.R.'s directions were to change as events were developing and which would affect everyone's life dramatically. Clouds of war were developing in Europe.

II
Change in Direction

After J.R. completed two semesters, Europe was at war and Pearl Harbor had occurred. He realized that before too long he would be drafted. He heard about a place called Quady in the state of Maine. Quady Village was an idea of Eleanor Roosevelt. A village dedicated to giving as many of the country's youth the skills needed to produce, maintain and operate the tools and instruments of war. Quady Village was a small village built to house and maintain workers who were going to build the first hydroelectric dam which was to produce electricity by harnessing the tides. The tides in Passamaquady Bay were about eleven feet. The project had to be abandoned due to the onset of World War II. Instead FDR and Congress decided to fund a technical school to teach aeronautical engineering and machinists. The village was to be run by the students. The village had a mayor, a council, a police force, fire dept., newspaper, etc., in fact all the required units of a small town. J.R. made an application to attend Quady and was accepted. When he arrived he was assigned a room in a one-story barracks that he shared with another fellow. After a short period of getting acquainted with the village J.R. along with the other new arrival was asked to report to a classroom for class assignment. J.R. was informed he would learn to be a machinist. J.R. objected and explained he came to Quady to learn Aeronautical Engineering. He was told that the Aeronautical Engineering class was closed since they had all the students they could accommodate. J.R. was very disappointed but could do nothing about it.

J.R. settled down to his environment in a very harsh Maine winter. There was a considerable amount of snow and the temperature got as low as thirty-two degrees below zero. The day that happened everyone was instructed to stay indoors and put on as much clothing as possible even though the heating units were working full blast.

One day after a number of days of snow which blanketed the village J.R. was told the barracks where he bunked was on fire. J.R. was in the machine shop that was an avenue block away from his barracks. He immediately dropped everything and ran as fast as he could to try to save his belongings. When he got there he found one of the boys lying on his stomach just outside the hallway that led from the lobby. The young boy was one of the firemen with a hose in his hand spraying the flames in the hallway. Along this hallway there were doors leading to the dormitory rooms. J.R.'s room was the first door. J.R. asked the fireman to move his hose over so that he could get into his room. The fireman said no one was permitted into a building that was on fire. J.R. said he wanted to save his belongings before the fire consumed them. The fireman relented and moved his hose. J.R. quickly entered the room and closed the door but almost immediately found himself in trouble. The room was full of smoke, choking him. J.R. took out his handkerchief, ran over to the sink and soaked it. He placed the handkerchief over his mouth and nose and put his belongings together and those of his roommate, opened the windows and threw them out. Then he took the bedding along with the beds and threw them out the window and jumped out the window onto the bed. The fire raged on in spite of the noble efforts of the firemen and J.R.'s dorm was gone along with the belongings of many of the other boys who lived there.

Now the problem was, where will they stay? This turned out very well as the councilmen immediately went to work to find places for each and every one that was affected. J.R. was very lucky; one of the councilmen invited him to stay in the building reserved for the council although he had to place his cot in the hallway outside the rooms on the second floor. An investigation by the detectives in the police department began as soon as the remains cooled down. It was determined that the fire was arson. Now the young inexperienced detective had to go to work and find the culprit. In a relatively short time they narrowed the search down to three possibilities. The three were invited to a meeting and they were told that they were suspected and that it won't be long before they knew who did it. This placed a great deal of pressure on the guilty one. The pressure worked and one of the three decided to run for it and stole one of the instructor's cars and made his way to Canada. The Canadian police were notified and very shortly caught the youth.

A few days later J.R. was invited to join the staff of the newspaper as a reporter. From time to time he submitted short articles he was assigned to cover. Aside from his reporting duties J.R. spent most of his spare time in the photo lab. The village had a great photo lab with a lot of expensive equipment. He took photos and developed, printed and enlarged them in the lab.

One day there was an announcement of an impending election for mayor in a few weeks. The mayor announced he would run for re-election and so who was going to run against him? The newspaper announced they would seek a suitable opponent. While the two groups were organizing their strategies a prizefight was announced. This was a very exciting event since there were few recreational evens. Prior to the fight the two opponents were working out daily. J.R. knew one of the prizefighters and took the occasion to photograph him and develop and enlarge a few prints of the picture for himself and the newspaper. Finally the evening arrived. Every single person in the village was there.

The noise was tremendous. The fight was hard fought but J.R.'s friend was outclassed by his handsome black opponent. About a week or so later the newspaper announced their candidate for mayor; of course it was the victorious prizefighter. They very quickly decided to print up cartoons on paper handouts. One of the editors asked J.R. if he would help hand out the cartoons. Since he was a reporter he felt he couldn't refuse. The next day while handing out the cartoons which blasted the mayor a councilmen came over to him and asked him how can he do this to the people who took him in and gave him a place to stay when he was in desperate need. Of course J.R. was very embarrassed. When the election was over and the votes were counted the champion prizefighter won and became mayor.

When the courses were completed J.R. was told if he wanted to, he could continue to learn about aircraft maintenance. There was a job working for the government in Harrisburg, Pennsylvania. J.R. agreed and signed up. Arrangements were made for a car pool and housing was provided by local people who had excess space in their homes, usually in their attic. They also provided meals. J.R.'s work began in a large aircraft hangar building which contained several airplanes. When J.R. arrived he was given a large toolbox filled with tools and what his first job was to be and again he was disappointed. His job was drilling out rivets on the plane's wing. It was tedious and boring but it was a new atmosphere and a new lifestyle and so J.R. decided to stick it out and see if it improved.

Harrisburg was a rather small old town that rolled up the sidewalks at night. There was little or nothing to do at night, but teenagers will always find some sort of mischief to occupy them. J.R.'s friends heard of a cathouse not too far away. They walked over together since they would never do this by themselves. One of the boys knocked on the door. A nice middle-aged woman answered the door and invited them in. They were ushered into a large living room full of mostly what seemed then elderly men sitting and impatiently waiting. The madam went around trying to occupy them during the wait. From time to time one of them was summoned upstairs.

At this point in time it was the second half of 1942. The war with Germany and Japan was ongoing since Pearl Harbor Dec. 7, 1941. J.R. at this point was nineteen years old and would soon be drafted since the draft was in effect for some time. J.R. knew that if he were drafted the Army would place him in the infantry. He wanted to be in the Army Air Corps. On Oct. 2, 1942 while in Harrisburg he enlisted in the Army Air Corps. This was shortly before his twentieth birthday. He was sent home and given two weeks to prepare himself for entering the service. He was ordered to report for duty on a specific date at an Army Air Force Corps in Harrisburg.

III

J.R.'s Adventures in the Army Air Force

Fortunately J.R.'s past experience away from Mom and the comforts of home (summer camp and Quady Village) served him well. The culture shock was not felt at all. The only problem he encountered was the discipline and the lack of freedom. In addition, he was not prepared for the many adventures, disappointments and dangers.

The first two days after J.R. reported for duty were very busy. There was the physical exam, the assignment of quarters and receiving O.D's (official dress) that included everything from head to toe and including two large barracks bags. When these two barracks bags were loaded with all the clothes and other possessions they were bulging and very heavy.

The following days were boring, waiting to be shipped out to a basic training camp. When the day finally came J.R. found it very difficult to lift the two barracks bags. Climbing on to the train was impossible. When it was J.R.'s turn to climb on to the train carrying his two barracks bags he just couldn't make the first step. The fellow behind him had to give him a shove in order for him to make it. Upon entering the train, lo and behold it was a Pullman car and J.R. was assigned to a private room. Each Pullman car had a private room on the back end of the car. It was shared with another soldier. The train had a dining car with tables and chairs and all the finery of a restaurant. What luxury! It was the best train ride of his Army career.

The trip was a long one. It was from Pennsylvania to Biloxi, Mississippi and Kiesler Field. Kiesler was a very large Army Air Force base. It had a lot of facilities that most other bases did not have. It had a large swimming pool and a place to go rowing. The negative side of the base was its personnel. The drill sergeants were tough and demanding. The first thing they demanded was a haircut (Marine style). J.R. at the time had a thick long head of hair and objected to a crew cut until he was warned not to test fate. After leaving the barbershop he felt like he was naked. Most of his day was spent marching or as they called it doing close order drill. In addition there were other tasks such as garbage collection, guard duty, K.P. (kitchen police), etc. This went on for seven days a week until one of the recruits objected and requested one day off on Sunday to attend church. Unbelievably the request was granted. What a feeling. J.R. didn't know what to do with himself for a full day without discipline.

When the basic training was completed now it was time for evaluation and assignment and then shipment to a new camp. All this took time because the Army was receiving more new recruits than they had places to keep them. This meant hurry up and wait. While he was waiting J.R. noted Kiesler Field had large aircraft hangars where mechanics worked on airplanes. J.R. felt that if he made some good contacts he may be assigned to Kiesler Field. But J .R. struck out. He was told that he didn't stand a chance getting a local assignment. After about two weeks of boring waiting, word was received that they were shipping out. Of course this was wartime and therefore everything that happened in the military was secret. They therefore were not told where they were going. In fact they were headed for a tent city outside of San Bernardino, California. These poor young kids did not know what they were about to experience both on the troop train and at the tent city. The troop train was a large one, consisting of day coaches with hard seats. The sleeping quarters were a day coach stripped of the seats with triple decked bunks installed. The mess hall was an empty railroad car that was normally used to ship commercial goods. The rail car was set up with large cans with a wooden board placed on top and used as a table to hold trays of food and large cooking pots. The boys would line up with their mess kits and file past the line of K.P.'s (kitchen police) doling out the food. Then they would return to their seats and eat without a table. When they were through they returned to the mess and discarded the remaining food into a large can and dipped the mess kit in a large can filled with boiling water. Little did the boys know they were headed for a camp where they would have to endure this for as long as they stayed at this camp.

Upon arrival at the tent city they were told that the purpose of this camp was for them to put an airfield that was under construction nearby in operating condition after construction was completed. In the meantime they had to familiarize themselves with their new home. They weren't there very long when they were told they had to build a bandstand and a seating area. It seems the Army Air Force decided to establish an Army Air Force band at the camp. In order to accomplish this the commanding officer went personally throughout the camp ordering every soldier he found to fall-in and accompany him to the site of the future outdoor theater where all the necessary equipment was unloaded. The work began about a few hours after supper and lasted till 3 a.m. when everyone was permitted to return to his tent to get some sleep.

The next day J.R. noticed a number of new men with musical instruments seating themselves on the stage. His curiosity got the better of him and he approached them and engaged them in conversation. "Where you from? I'm from New York and played with the Dorsey Band." Another fellow said he was also from New York and played for the Goodman Band. It seemed they all came from the top bands. In addition to having a talented group of musicians to entertain them they soon were being entertained by Hollywood talent brought in by Dorothy Lamour, the actress who did all the road shows with Bob Hope. It seems that the adjutant to the commanding officer was engaged to Dorothy Lamour at the time. The entertainment helped to make this miserable camp tolerable.

The weather during the day was generally good, but sunset to sunrise it was cool and damp. When J.R. awoke in the morning and put on his coveralls it felt as if it were just soaked in a bucket of water. One evening J.R. developed a fever and felt very sick. He asked a few of his buddies if there was an infirmary or doctor in the camp. He was told he would have to wait till sick call the next morning. One of his friends was a cowboy in civilian life. He told J.R. to go to bed and he will help him fall asleep. His friend pulled out a guitar from under his bunk and started to play and sing cowboy songs. J.R. was asleep in minutes. The next morning J.R. went to the first-aid tent on the company street that had a line of men waiting to go to sick call and he got on line. After a long wait he was called into the tent. There were several men seated, one of whom examined each person entering the tent. The examiner thrust a thermometer in J.R.'s mouth. When he read the thermometer he told J.R. his temperature was 104. J.R. was told to go back to his tent and pack up his belongings and turn in his bedding and return to await the ambulance. J.R. staggered back to his tent but couldn't do anything. In fact he had trouble standing. His tent mate told him to go back, that they will take care of everything for him. He returned and was told to sit next to a potbelly stove and wait for the ambulance. Since J.R. was burning up with fever, sitting next to a red hot potbelly stove was a bad idea. He decided to sit outside on the damp ground. The ambulance turned out to be a jeep. Of those who were going to the hospital no one wanted to sit next to J.R. therefore he was told to sit in the back seat. J.R. spent about a week and a half in the hospital until his fever was under control and then he returned to duty.

A few days after being released one of J.R.'s tent mates asked him if he wanted to join him and go to San Bernardino. J.R. thought it would be great to get away from the hellhole even for a little while. All his buddy had in mind was a drunken binge. When they arrived at the bus stop in town they headed for the closest bar. Although J.R. was not a drinker he made no objection because of his disillusion with the Army Air Corps. They sat at the bar until J.R. felt hungry. The bartender told J.R. they did not serve food but there was a store across the street where you could get something to eat. J.R. left and went across the street and found a Mexican chili joint. J.R. asked the man if they had anything else; he said no and so he ordered a bowl. J.R. started to eat the chili and suddenly realized it was *very* hot chili. J.R. ran out of the store with his mouth on fire. He ran back to the bar and asked for a glass of water to put out the flames. Before he and his friend Mike left they bought a bottle of whiskey. By then they were thoroughly drunk. They worked their way back to the bus stop but found they had missed the last bus to the camp. What could they do? They sat down on the curb. At around midnight the M.P.s made their roundup of the drunks who had passes to be around town. They of course found Mike and J.R. and helped them into the jeep. They were dropped off at the entrance to the camp. J.R. staggered to the entrance where there were two M.P.s who usually checked all the passes or I.D.s. J.R. and Mike were so drunk they didn't bother. As J.R. staggered through the entrance he dropped the liquor bottle that he had put under his belt. The M.P.s smiled but said nothing. The next day J.R.'s attention was directed toward a small prison that was just built in front of the camp near the entrance. It was a chain link fence about twenty feet by ten feet with a tent inside. It seems there was a nasty drunk in there yelling obscenities at the C.O. (commanding officer) who was passing by. The C.O. took off his jacket and attempted to go into the jail but was stopped by the armed guard who was on duty.

A few days later they were notified they were shipping out to a new camp. The new camp turned out to be a much worse camp. It was an abandoned Japanese internment camp. The Japanese were sent east because a Japanese invasion of the west coast was expected. This camp was located outside of San Francisco on the site of the Tan Feran racetrack. It was an absolute disgrace that the Army Air Force would treat young men in this irresponsible way. When they got there they found a place that looked like a concentration camp. It had elevated guard posts at the four corners of the fenced area with barbed wire on the top. The water system was sabotaged by the Japanese before they were shipped east. The showers were built for the short stature of the Japanese. Due to the prevailing weather in San Francisco the ground was muddy and the mud was tracked into the barracks, mess hall and anywhere you went. In addition they shipped in so many men into this camp that the bunks were one next to the other with no space between bunks. With conditions like these it was inevitable for sickness to follow and follow it did. Not only did one after another get sick but the boys began to die one after another of spinal meningitis, pneumonia, etc. The numbers became alarming so much so that an inspector general was sent to the camp. Of course before he arrived everything was made spick and span.

Shortly after arriving at the prison, or at least that was what everyone felt it was, J.R. developed laryngitis. He could only speak in a whisper. During the morning line-up there was a roll call. J.R. would get out of line and station himself behind the first sergeant. When his name was called he would tap the first sergeant on the shoulder. All the fellows in his unit thought he had a permanent affliction. J.R. went on sick call and when he saw the doctor he was told that there was nothing he could do. J.R. asked him to recommend his transfer. The doctor said he could not do it.

Due to the impossible conditions caused by the muddy roads around the camp everyone was ordered to join large work gangs to dig up the earth around the barracks. Since J.R. had largyngitis this activity was the worst thing that could happen to him. But just as J.R. was cursing his situation a fellow came along and asked for volunteers with a good handwriting. Although J.R. had a terrible handwriting he felt that anything would be better than this. Only three or four fellows raised their hands. It was well-known that you should never volunteer because you will wind up with a very unpleasant if not dangerous job. The volunteers were taken to a barracks that had mail bags piled to the ceiling in one of the buildings and there was another barracks full of mailbags. The mailbag contained mail for the men that were transferred and therefore undeliverable. The volunteers were given a desk, a bag of mail and several pages of names and addresses and instructed to redirect the mail. This was heaven sent, sitting in a building with a potbelly stove, nice and comfortable doing an easy job. This gave J.R. a great deal of satisfaction, at last he was doing something of importance. After two weeks of redirecting mail J.R. started to get his voice back. The laryngitis was gone. All his buddies were shocked when they heard J.R. talk normally.

IV

Could Conditions Possibly Improve?

About a week or so later in accordance with the order to evacuate the camp some of the men started to leave. There was a rail line adjacent to the camp. A train pulled in and a designated group of men were told to board the train. The entire camp was on alert to be prepared to leave on a moment's notice. One day J.R. was busy redirecting mail when one of the other fellows doing the same work came into the building and told J.R. that everyone in his barracks was already on the train and that he might be left behind. J.R. got up and ran as fast as he could to his barracks. He tied his barracks bags together, threw them over his shoulder and ran to the train. He was relieved that he caught the train. After disposing of his bags he found himself a seat. This troop train was one of the most uncomfortable trips J.R. had to endure. The chow line ran through a cattle car in which there were men behind large pots, etc. from which they served the chow of the day to the G.I.s in their mess kits. The G.I.s were randomly selected to work as K.P.s. J.R. was never picked. The G.I.s slept in a car that was converted by removing the seats and replacing them with triple-decked bunks.

During the trip J.R. was told they were going to Congorie, South Carolina. He didn't believe the rumor. Whoever heard of a town called Congorie? "We must be going overseas, maybe to Africa," he said.

As it turned out there was town called Congorie immediately next to a newly built Army Air Force Base. J.R. and the others were sent there to organize and set up the newly constructed air base. The base was built like most permanent air bases with aircraft hangars, a landing strip, a mess hall and barracks. J.R. could hardly believe his good luck after surviving the last two camps.

After his assignment to a barracks and getting himself settled he was assigned to work in the kitchen with the cooks but as a coal stoker of the stove. It was a rather easy job and better than K.P. (kitchen police). It seems the Commanding Officer of the base was a character. One day when he was running around in his jeep he saw a group of men sitting and smoking outside of one of the hangars. He stopped his jeep and bawled the men out for goofing off. The supervising sergeant spoke up and explained that they worked hard all morning and deserved a break. The C.O. ordered them back to work. One night, at about 2 a.m., the C.O. ordered everyone on an alert. They had to get up, dress and race outside to practice protecting the base. Since there was no enemy, it was an action in futility. This and many other actions convinced the other officers that they had to get rid of this C.O. somehow.

One day J.R. was informed by the cook that there was to be an inspection the next day. He was told to take a ham rind and wipe the entire stove including the back of the stove. That seemed strange to J.R. and he asked why the back of the stove? The cook said that this C.O. had a habit of inspecting with a white glove. Finally the moment came. The C.O. entered the kitchen; they were all standing at attention at their stations. After inspecting one by one the different parts of the kitchen he came over to J.R.'s station, the stove. He looked over the stove, it looked shiny clean. He then put his white-gloved hand in the back of the stove expecting to find some dirt but instead when he withdrew his hand and looked at the glove it was loaded with grease. He shouted, "What the hell is this?" The cook explained that is the prescribed method of keeping a stove clean and in good shape. The C.O. stormed out in anger. He knew he had been had.

One day the C.O. arrived at the kitchen and entered the food locker and removed a ham, some butter, cheese, etc. and placed them in the trunk of his personal car. The cook immediately informed the officer in charge of the mess hall and kitchen. The mess officer called the M.P.s. When the C.O. arrived at the entrance of the camp he was stopped and asked to open his trunk. The M.P.s found the food and confiscated them and sent him on his way. A week later the C.O. received orders to report to Washington for reassignment.

A few days later J.R. was given the job as head of message center. What a break! He was given a small motor scooter with a large box on the front. He had to travel to base headquarters which was several miles away, on the other side of the air base. He also had to visit three warehouses to pick up or deliver whatever was required. One day J.R. came speeding back to the orderly room, stopping his motor scooter short and sliding to a stop on the sand. The Commanding Officer yelled out, "Come in to my office immediately." The C.O. was a man in his thirties or early forties and to J.R. very fatherly. The C.O. asked J.R., did he know that he received a speeding ticket? He said, no, he wasn't stopped. The C.O. said he received a ticket from a M.P. driving his private car. He asked J.R., "How could you be going fifty miles an hour in that little motor scooter?" J.R. explained that on the way back from headquarters there is a steep hill but he didn't believe he could be going fifty miles an hour speeding down that hill on the scooter.

About a month later when J.R. was making his rounds at one of the warehouses a sergeant gave J.R. a very large milk can and asked him to fill it with gas for a vehicle he named and gave him the I.D. number. J.R. obediently went to the gas pump and the corporal filled out a form. After the milk can was filled J.R. signed the form. He returned the milk can to the sergeant and forgot about the whole thing. A few days later J.R. saw a M.P. with a rifle in hand march off the sergeant. J.R. thought nothing of it until he was called into the work detail officer's office. He showed J.R. a gas receipt and asked him if it was his signature. J.R. readily admitted he signed the receipt and obtained the gas. The lieutenant explained to J.R. that he obtained gas for a vehicle that uses diesel fuel, not gas. He said that J.R. was stealing gas and could go to jail for this. J.R. explained that he was ordered to obtain the gas by the sergeant and he did not know the vehicle used diesel fuel. While the sergeant resided in jail the company doctor was selected to make an inquiry. A few days later J.R. was asked to report to the doctor. When he reported to the doctor he was immediately asked if he was willing to give the sergeant a recommendation of good character. J.R. responded immediately saying, "Would you give a recommendation of good character to a sergeant who ordered you to obtain gas for him under false pretenses?" Without another word he told J.R. to leave.

One day J.R. along with the rest of the men had to take a written examination. They were not told what the exam was all about. J.R. did the best he could and then promptly forgot all about it. Some weeks later a list appeared on the bulletin board and J.R.'s name was among them. J.R. found out that the list resulted from the exam they took. Everyone in the army, no matter what branch of service, were given this exam to determine who was to be picked to go to college. J.R. panicked; he could not understand why they would pick a soldier out of the army to go to college while a war for survival was in progress. He felt that if he left the Army Air Force for college he would wind up in the infantry—exactly what he hoped to avoid by enlisting in the Air Force. He felt the only choice he had to avoid going to college was to get a leave of absence. J.R. rushed to the orderly room and asked the first sergeant if he could see the C.O. (Commanding Officer). The sergeant went into the C.O.'s office and got permission. J.R. went in and saluted, and began his pitch, but before he could say more than a few words the C.O. stopped him. The C.O. said, "Soldier, do you still have the manual you received when you entered the service?" J.R. replied, "It's in the bottom of my barracks bag." The C.O. dismissed J.R. and told him to return when he read his manual. J.R. left and asked the sergeant what was the problem? He told J.R. that after he saluted he should ask permission to speak to the C.O. J.R. returned and went through the correct procedure and then asked for a furlough explaining he had not been home since he enlisted. Much to his surprise the C.O. said since he expected to give out furloughs to all who were eligible he will approve J.R.'s. J.R. was shocked but also delighted. He was told to return in the morning and he would have his papers. J.R. could hardly believe his good luck.

The next morning he received his pass and left the air base for home. When he returned from leave two weeks later he was walking down the company street when he suddenly met the lieutenant in charge of the college selection committee. The lieutenant asked J.R. why he didn't report to the committee as ordered. The lieutenant explained that the order was posted two weeks ago. J.R. responded by saying he was away on leave. The lieutenant promptly ordered J.R. to report to him the next morning. It was then J.R. found out everyone was ordered to attend a gas drill. J.R. was on the horns of a dilemma. Where should he report?

He went to the First Sergeant and explained his predicament. The First Sergeant explained to J.R. that the Commanding Officer who ordered the gas drill has rank over the lieutenant and he had better show up at the gas drill. J.R. was delighted—anything to avoid the college committee. J.R. showed up the next morning at the gas drill that was being held in a remote part of the base. His gas mask in tow, J.R. got in a long line outside of a large trailer. After waiting a short while the lieutenant in charge of the selection committee showed up in a jeep. The lieutenant ordered J.R. into his jeep. He then drove to where the committee was meeting.

Before appearing in front of the board J.R. was told to select the subjects he would prefer studying. Some of the subjects were languages, engineering and psychology. When J.R. appeared before the board he was asked to choose. J.R. had no objection to spending time studying in college, instead of the boredom, incarceration and some of the former camps J.R. survived. He was fearful of winding up in the infantry or worse. He told the board that the flunked French in high school and therefore languages were out. He said he wasn't so good in math so engineering was out. He said psychology sounded interesting; he therefore selected psychology. When J.R. left he hoped his response would kill his selection. He returned to the line of the gas drill. When he reached the trailer he was told to put on his gas mask before entering. It seems the trailer was loaded with tear gas. J.R. entered the trailer and as soon as the last fellow left he was told to remove his gas mask. The experience was awful. J.R. rushed to exit the trailer.

A few weeks later J.R. received orders to proceed to Clemson College. When he arrived he asked if this was the college he would attend. He was told that this was just temporary and that they will be told which college they will be going to. In the meantime it was sit around and wait. After two days of sitting and waiting J.R. began looking for something to release the boredom. The next afternoon J.R. decided to take a stroll to the adjacent town in spite of strict instructions not to leave the dormitory. Before leaving J.R. asked his friends if they cared to join him. Three of his friends decided to join him. The four proceeded down the stairs from the dorm that was located on the second floor of the large building with J.R. in the lead. When he opened the door to exit the building he noticed a student doing guard duty with a wooden gun in hand. J.R waited until the student rounded the corner and then signaled the others to follow him. J.R. very quickly exited the building and ran to a small woodlands about 500 feet from the building. As soon as they cleared the woodlands they arrived at the edge of town. They enjoyed their freedom, taking a slow stroll through this small town. At the approach of sunset J.R. decided to make the way back. This turned out to be the hardest part of their adventure. When they reached the strand of trees J.R. told his friends to wait while he reconnoitered. J.R. proceeded to the edge of the woodland and checked to see if the cadets doing guard duty were anywhere in sight. When he spotted the guard he waited till he was out of sight. He then called his friends to follow him. J.R. very quickly ran to the back of the building. When he was about to open the rear entrance door he noticed a civilian sitting in an alcove outside the entrance. J.R. just ignored the night watchman and quickly entered the building and bounded up the stairs with his buddies just behind him. He entered his room; his bed was immediately to the left of the entrance. J.R. straightened out the mattress which was rolled up as if no one was ever using this bed. He threw his blanket over the bed and jumped into the bed covering himself up and laying his head on the pillow as if fast asleep. In a few minutes he heard the sentry bounding up the stairs and then looking in each room. The sentry then came to J.R.'s room and looked in. Everything looked normal. He looked into room after room but he never found the offending soldiers.

The following week they received their orders. They traveled by train to Washington, D.C. and then bused to College Park, Maryland and Maryland University with its beautiful campus. When they arrived they were introduced to the C.O. and his first sergeant. They were informed that this was ASTP (Army Specialized Training Program) and that they will be studying Engineering. They were, however, not taking the usual four-year course. The professors tried to explain to the military that two years would not work. Naturally, the military knew best. In fact, some professors quit rather than teach an accelerated course. Since it was an engineering course and in addition an accelerated course, J.R. knew he had no chance at all of passing. But, orders are orders and so he decided to do his best. Besides the curriculum the students were soldiers, in fact, cadets. What it meant was besides the usual army discipline they had to live up to a higher standard of discipline. Each cadet shared a room with another cadet. Each day one of the cadets had the responsibility of the cleanliness of the room. Each bed had to be made perfectly and shoes shined. Every morning before breakfast there was flag raising. The cadets fell out, and lined up dressed perfectly. Any infraction of the rules, no matter how small, meant demerits. The number of demerits determined the severity of the punishment. Each day one of the cadets in each room had the responsibility for the cleanliness of the room. One day when it was J.R.'s turn he forgot to do his job. The next day the number of demerits was posted on the bulletin board. The punishment was Cadet O.D. (Officer of the Day) over the weekend while the others received a leave of absence to visit Wasington, D.C. This punishment wasn't so bad, others were not so lucky. One cadet had to walk back and forth in an enclosed area with a backpack full of bricks for a long period. The curriculum was very difficult. Besides History and English composition, there was Chemistry, Physics and two advance math courses and physical education. Phys-ed consisted of boxing lessons, judo or exercises such as a three-mile jog followed by a five-mile jog the following week. The class after phys-ed was physics. Physics was J.R.'s nemesis. In addition to a lecture class in physics there was a physics laboratory class. In this class they were taught physics principles and shown a lab test that proved it. The student had to recreate the experiment and write an explanation showing a drawing of the experiment. J.R. liked the lab class and was always the last to leave, wanting to complete an accurate account of the experiment. He received a perfect mark for each session.

Mid-term exams came in half the normal time. At least 90 percent failed and had to see the Chancellor along with the Commanding Officer. A long line was formed and one by one each cadet came before them and explained why they failed and what they expected to do about it.

Between the mid-term exams and final exams at least ten students left to return to army service. When they started there were about 300 students; at the time of final exams there were only 100 students left. As the final exams approached all the students were studying long and hard.

With the approval of his roommates J.R. asked for permission to keep his room lights on after lights out in order to put in an extra hour or two to study. Finally the date and time of the final exam for each course was posted. In addition to the difficulties J.R. had with physics and chemistry he also had trouble with one of the advanced math classes. When the class was starting J.R. sat in the front row and was doing well. After two or three weeks the teacher protested the accelerated curriculum and left. The new teacher decided to assign a new seating arrangement. J.R. wound up in the last row. After the change the students in the back of the room were always clowning around which was a distraction. J.R. began to flunk all the daily exams. When the final exams were announced it was on the day of a religious holiday and J.R. decided to spend the holiday at home. J.R. informed the instructor who agreed to give the exam on the day J.R. was scheduled to leave for home. He worked away at the two math exams diligently. He completed the first math exam but couldn't complete the second. He had to catch a train, he therefore had to leave the last two questions unanswered. When he returned J.R. met his math teacher who told him he just couldn't understand him. The teacher said that J.R. was failing the course all along because he failed all the exams he gave him except the two final exams and those two he passed with very high marks. The teacher could not understand him. When all the marks were in, J.R. was informed that he passed all the exams except chemistry and physics which he received a doubtful. This meant he did not fail any course. At this juncture all those who passed all their courses were those who had taken the courses before. They were given two weeks leave of absence so they could go home. J.R. was given a choice of remaining at the university and take the two tests over again or leave with those who failed.

V
Back to the Army Air Corps

J.R. was convinced from the beginning of the failure of the ASTP. He therefore chose to leave after returning from a two week leave of absence. When he returned he received orders to travel to an Advanced Basic Training Camp in North Carolina. The army's reward for failure. All this was at a time when a world war was in progress.

The Advanced Basic Training consisted of more of the usual marching, rifle marksmanship, guard duty, etc. The only difference was their obstacle course. The trainer was required to climb out of a slit trench, which was ten-foot deep, under fire from two old WWI .30-caliber machine guns firing from the two front corners of the obstacle course. Then he had to crawl under barbed wire past shell holes that exploded as they passed. A very hair-raising event. Fortunately no one was killed or injured in the process.

When the "training" was over J.R. received orders to proceed to Buckley Field, Denver, Colorado. At Buckley, J.R. was to attend an armament school. It wasn't what J.R. wanted but it was an improvement over his previous military experience. This school taught the .50-caliber machine gun, bombs, etc. Buckley Field was just outside of Denver which was a very nice old town. The people were very nice and friendly. Buckley Field was a very nice base.

It had all the comfortable facilities, a P.X. (general store) where you can buy almost anything, barracks, mess hall, etc. The only thing J.R. didn't like was the winter weather. It snowed heavily and had temperatures down to thirty-two below zero. One very cold evening J.R. entered his barracks preparing to go to sleep. He noticed the pot bellied stove in the middle of the barracks was working on a very low flame. Anticipating an extra cold evening he decided to do something about the lack of heat. Outside there was a coal shed holding large chunks of coal. J.R. went outside and kept taking chunks until the stove was full of coal. Later that evening when the small fire at the bottom of the stove got to the large chunks the stove glowed from top to bottom and the barracks was very comfortable.

Later that winter J.R. came down with a terrible cold and a high fever and landed in the base hospital. After a few days the fever eased and the full-blown cold eased but he developed laryngitis just a few days before Christmas. At that time in Buckley Field they always issued leave of absence. When J.R. asked the doctor to be released from the hospital the doctor said, "When you get rid of the laryngitis." J.R. started working diligently to inhale medication inserted in water that was placed on a hot plate. He used this regimen three times a day. On the day before Christmas he begged the doctor to release him. Since there was a good improvement of his condition the doctor consented. The first thing J.R. did when he went to Denver was to find the best restaurant in town and order the best steak.

The last part of his training as an armorer was a visit to the firing range. There was a P–40 fighter plane rigged with a .20-mm cannon. The instructor loaded the cannon with a shell and asked J.R. if he would like to fire the weapon, which he promptly did. The next exhibit was the malfunction range. It consisted of a number of .50-caliber machine guns placed every so often around a semi-circle. Each gun had something wrong with it. The instructor went from gun to gun explaining what was wrong. One of the guns was called a runaway gun. When it was fired it did not stop automatically. The students had to learn how to stop the runaway gun. While the instructor was stripping one of the guns he gave J.R. the main part of the firing mechanism that was a large bar of steel about a foot long and about a few inches thick. It was quite heavy. Suddenly the runaway gun that was behind J.R. went off. It startled J.R. so much that the steel block flew up in the air and then down to the ground. The sound of a .50-caliber machine gun is quite loud.

One of the last items of instruction was a walk through a building with a number of machine gun turrets that appeared to be hanging from the ceiling. Instead of teaching them the function of turrets the instructor just pointed out each turret and named them. When the course was completed each student was awarded corporal promotion and given stripes that had to be sewn on the sleeves of their shirts and jackets. But in spite of the promotion J.R. was not impressed. He wasn't happy being an armorer. He felt the only way he could really contribute was to sign up to be a pilot. He signed up and was given a battery of tests, most of which were physical. One was depth perception, another was peripheral vision. He passed all the tests and was accepted. He was promptly shipped to Harlingen, Texas located in the northern part of Texas near the panhandle. This was after spending the winter in Denver. They were sending J.R. to spend the summer in the heat of Texas, where they have the worst tasting water in the U.S.A. The G.I. had to drink soft drinks if and when they were able to get them. Cadet basic training was tough enough without having it in the summer in Texas.

One day the cadets were marched out to the parade ground and given pistols to practice the handling and aiming of the pistol. While practice was going on a sandstorm popped up. The practice continued but it became so severe that you could hardly see anything and the blowing sand was stinging their hands and faces. Finally the instructor called a halt. When they got back to the barracks they found a fine layer of sand over everything.

A week later J.R. received a letter from his mother informing him his grandmother was gravely ill in the hospital in Kansas City, MO and if he is able to see her he should. J.R. asked and was fortunate to receive permission and received a ten-day pass. The next day he left camp for the railroad station. While waiting for the train J.R. decided to have a beer. Thirst was always with you when stationed at Harlingen, Texas. After a few sips J.R. noticed the beer seemed very strong. It seemed the alcohol content was much higher than he was used to. When the train arrived J.R. got on with a group of cowboys. They were a rough bunch from their talk. They were obviously drinking and from their looks J.R. thought they were going to Kansas City to pick up their pay for the sale of their cattle.

When he arrived in K.C. he took a cab to his uncle's factory. When he arrived his uncle greeted him and gave him a tour of the tie factory. Of course there were a lot of girls working with the sewing machines. The girls started to whistle as J.R. passed by in his Air Force uniform. Uncle Is took J.R. to the hospital to visit his grandmother. When he entered her room grandma remarked, "Who is the shvatza?" Is laughed and explained that "He's Gussie's son." Grandma motioned J.R. to come closer. She told J.R. that the hospital is starving her to save money. J.R. repeated what grandma said to Uncle Is who explained that she was critical with diabetes and therefore on a low calorie diet.

From the hospital they went to visit Uncle Abe and while there he asked Abe to entertain J.R. with his violin. Abe was once a child prodigy. He made a noble attempt to play as he had not played in many years. They then left to visit Uncle Jack. When they arrived he took them to the back of a one-family home where there was a large dog house. Uncle Jack told J.R. that is where he is living and told J.R. to crawl inside. When J.R. crawled inside he noticed a bear rug on the floor. After examining Uncle Jack's unique abode Jack asked J.R. if he would like to go horseback riding. J.R. agreed and Jack brought J.R. to a garage where he kept his wild horse he was training. When they approached the garage the horse started to kick the structure. Jack asked J.R. if he wanted to ride his horse. J.R. said no thank you. Jack then got J.R. another horse from a nearby stable and they rode off along the plains of Missouri.

When J.R. completed his stay he started his trip back to Harlingen. Since he still had some time on his ten-day pass J.R. stopped in Omaha, Nebraska. After looking around town he decided to try the U.S.O. since there was always something going on to entertain the servicemen. While J.R. was enjoying the hospitality available an announcement was made. Anyone of Jewish faith who needs a place to stay overnight, a family is waiting to hear from you. Since J.R. did not know where he would stay or where to find a place to stay overnight he gladly accepted the mother's hospitality. The nice-looking mother took J.R. to her home and family not knowing the character of J.R. She gave J.R. her son's room who was serving in the Navy. At the supper table he was treated as if he were the family's son. The conversation over the supper table was genuine and not artificial to hide family secrets. The food was excellent. When J.R. left for camp he couldn't thank them enough. He thoroughly enjoyed their company.

Back at camp the next day the cadets went to the firing range to test their ability to fire a pistol. The object was to hit a target that was the outline of a man standing about fifty feet away. Each cadet stood facing his own target. When the instructor stood in front of J.R. his pistol was carelessly pointing at the instructor. The instructor had a riding crop that he placed under the barrel of the gun and slowly lifted the barrel of the gun into the air instructing J.R. how to hold a loaded gun. Before firing the gun at the target, the target was facing sideways. When the cadets were ordered to fire the target was facing the cadets. They were told when ordered to fire. They were told to fire all five rounds in rapid succession. Since they were firing a .45-caliber pistol the kickback was great and therefore after each shot the gun had to be re-aimed.

After a short set of instructions the officer in charge yelled, "Ready." J.R., instead of holding his pistol up, aimed it at the edge of the target. The target was then turned facing the cadets. The voice again shouted, "Aim, fire." J.R. did very well, all his rounds hit the target. The next day the officer in charge called the cadets together informally. He told them he received a telegram from Hap Arnold, the general at the head of the Air Force. It said the Air Force had all the pilots they needed and therefore the cadets would not be going to pilot training. The Air Force needs gunners for their bombers. J.R. was upset. He shouted, "It's unfair." After two years of military service, his *only* hope was cadets and becoming a pilot and that hope was gone. The next week he was on a troop train going to an aerial gunnery school on the bottom of Texas on the shore of the Rio Grande across from Matamoras, Mexico.

VI
Back to School "Aerial Gunnery"

This school was a unique experience for J.R. The purpose of the school was to teach future gunners for bombers to shoot at high-speed targets such as enemy fighter planes. The powers that be, decided to start these students at shotgun shooting. This consisted of shooting at clay disks called pigeons. Two days of this and J.R. graduated to another shooting range that consisted of a large oval track in which trucks with platforms on the back road all around. The platform had an iron ring about three feet high where the students stand inside and fire at clay pigeons tossed from wooden towers strategically placed around the track. When the truck with the instructor and student passed over a cable placed across the track it triggered the machine that tossed the pigeon. The truck moved down the track at thirty miles an hour. Shooting at a small clay pigeon from the back of a truck going thirty miles an hour was no easy task. J.R. loved the challenge. After a week of shotgun shooting J.R. was shocked to notice at the end of the day when he took his shirt off and looked in the mirror the area of his chest and arm on the right side was black and blue. The recoil of the shotgun was pounding his chest. When J.R. completed his shotgun practice he had to wait for the other students to complete their practice. Since he was bored he volunteered to drive the truck around the track so the other students could complete their practice. J.R. had a G.I. driver's license. The office in charge gave one of the drivers a break and allowed J.R. to drive. J.R. jumped behind the wheel and waited for the instructor and student to climb on back. Then he took off down the track. However, instead of going 30 miles an hour, he went 40 miles an hour. It's hard enough to shoot a shotgun at a moving target at thirty miles an hour let alone at 40 miles an hour. The officer in charge stopped J.R. and bawled him out. He said if he didn't drive at thirty miles an hour he would ground him. J.R. thereafter made sure he went thirty miles an hour!

J.R. received his driver's license in one of his previous camps. It seems in this camp they were short of truck drivers and so they made an announcement that they were giving driver tests for all those who were interested. J.R. felt he wouldn't mind driving any vehicle any time he wasn't engaged. J.R. showed up at the place indicated along with five or six other G.I.s. There was an instructor with a 2.5-ton truck at the location. The instructor asked J.R. to get in the truck while he gave instruction to the rest of the group. J.R. was glad to get the time to examine the clutch that he would have to use. The clutch had three stick shifts. One was the main shift, the other two were on the floor and were very short. J.R. also noticed a plate on the dashboard indicating how the shift worked. In a few minutes the instructor jumped into the truck next to J.R. and said let's go! J.R. turned on the motor and asked where to? He was told to go straight ahead until he got to a roadway on the right and then to drive down that road. The road was very intimidating since it was very narrow, especially for a truck. In addition, the road had a steep embankment on both sides and had a sharp "S" turn.

J.R. shifted the gear and double clutched and off they

went. When he got to the side road he swung onto it. After entering the "S" turn the instructor told J.R. to shift into low gear. While still moving ahead he bent down under the dash to reach the low gear. He double clutched but it didn't respond. He double clutched again and the clutch engaged. The instructor asked J.R. to engage to low gear. This time the gear did not engage and the truck got dangerously close to the edge of the road because J.R. could not see where he was going. The instructor got scared and shouted, "O.K., forget about it. Back the truck out of this road." This order boggled J.R.'s mind. J.R. thought, *How in the hell am I going to back this truck through the "S" turn on this narrow road without killing both of us*? Well, orders are orders. J.R. shifted into reverse and started back. How he made it he would never know.

After shotgun shooting there were other interesting teaching skills. One day they were taken to a unique shooting range. It consisted of a number of .50-caliber machine guns lined up in front of a railroad track with a jeep riding the rails with a large cloth target mounted on it. The jeep kept riding down the rails while the students kept shooting at the target with different colored bullets. When J.R. arrived he was told to take a box of ammunition and place it next to one of the guns. The box must have weighed 100 lbs. J.R. struggled to lift the box. He managed the task with a super effort. J.R. did not do well.

The next day they were taken to a curious-looking building. It was in the shape of a large ball. Upon entering the building they found it was a projection studio. One side of the room was a large white screen; on the other side there were four or five projection rooms. In front of the screen there was a platform with a small unique seat that could move in any direction. J.R. was selected to be guineas pig number one. J.R. got in the unique seat and strapped himself in. Attached to the moveable seat was a wooden gun that projected a light in the form of a white dot on the screen. Of course, the object was to shoot down an evading fighter plane projected on the screen. The instructor ordered the film to begin. The four or five cameras sprang to life. The screen showed the tail turret of a bomber in action flying to a target. The projection on the screen was so real that J.R. was transported into that turret. Suddenly a German fighter plane appeared attacking his plane. It was a breathtaking sight. It was so realistic that if he were not strapped to his seat he would be on the floor. The shock threw his aim off and he missed the plane. He only got one chance because there were a number of classmates waiting.

Aside from learning the art of aerial gunnery there was military discipline. That is lining up, marching and parades. After completing the course they were qualified aerial gunners. To celebrate the commanding officer ordered a parade. J.R.'s unit was told the best unit would get a pass to go to Matamoras, Mexico. As J.R.'s unit lined up outside the parade grounds waiting their turn to march past the reviewing stand, the terrible heat started to get to the men. Suddenly some of them started to faint and fall to the ground. There were so many lying on the ground that there weren't enough first aid people to cart them off. The rest of the men marched off. The next day J.R.'s unit was notified they won the contest and they all received their pass. The trip to Matamoras was quite an adventure. It was a crude Mexican town but with a lot of interesting things to see. First there was the usual tourist trap, which was a very large tent covering more than two dozen merchants selling all sorts of items for the tourists. J.R. examined the merchandise and even bargained with one of the merchants for an item to be sent home. Then he marched on in his tour of

Matamoras. Of course in this dusty, ugly town there was a red light district. Incidentally, J.R. brought his camera with him and was snapping pictures throughout his walk around town. Before he left camp one of the officers warned the group not to drink anything unless it was in a can. They were also told that films would not be permitted to be brought across the border. J.R. felt he could conceal the film and get it across. As J.R. approached the bridge across the Rio Grande that was totally dry, he noticed a cart with large slices of meat laid out on the cart with swarms of flies on the meat. It was a disgusting sight.

Well now, there was nothing to do but wait for a new assignment to a bomber base where they will practice. J.R. had a hard time waiting when they received corporal stripes and shoulder patches. J.R. decided to overcome boredom by going into business. To insure they would be busy until they had to leave, J.R. decided to just charge one dollar to sew on the stripes and patches. He asked a friend to do the ironing and he would do the sewing.

After a wait of weeks they received their orders. It seemed the officer making the assignment orders used his head (a rare occurrence). The assignments were made in accordance with where each man lived. The purpose was to assign an airman to an airbase nearest his home. J.R., therefore, was sent to Westover Army Air Force Base located outside of Holioke, Mass. Westover was a B-24 (heavy bomber) base. It was used to train bomber crews for combat flying. The purpose of each flight was to train each member of the crew not only to improve their skill but to work together as a team.

VII

J.R. Advances into the Wild Blue

When they arrived at Westover all they knew was they were going to fly as a member of a B-24 crew. Most if not all of them never flew in any plane before. There was nothing much to do now but wait for an assignment which as usual is a long wait. In the meantime they decided to check out the facilities of the airbase especially the P.X. (Post Exchange). As the days went by and they made themselves at home boredom set in. That's when rumors start to pop up. The word that got around was that if they didn't fly soon they would lose their flying pay. J.R.'s friends decided to go to the flight line and ask for a ride. When J.R.'s turn came he was told the plane was going up for a prop test. When he heard this he felt it would be like a walk in the park. The pilot came over to J.R. and asked J.R. to follow him. They picked up their parachutes and walked a short distance to the plane. After boarding the plane, which was a twin seat training plane, the pilot started the engine. The plane proceeded to the runway. After the pilot received permission to take off he rolled down the runway, picking up speed as he went. The plane lifted off and very slowly gained altitude.

When he arrived at the proper altitude and location he started a series of acrobatics. First he turned the plane upside down. J.R. was amused. The pilot then started a few shallow dives. J.R. was enjoying the ride so far. Then the pilot went into a very steep dive. The "G" forces were incredibly strong when the pilot started to pull out of the dive. The feeling was unbelievable. It felt as if his stomach was wrapped around his backbone and his cheeks were being pushed to the back of his mouth. It was as if an elephant was sitting on him. J.R. passed out for a second or two and then rapidly recovered. But that was not the end. The plane then went back up to about six or seven thousand feet. Since the pilot did not scare J.R. sufficiently he had one more stunt to try.

He brought the plane straight up as if to climb to the stars until the motor stalled. Then the nose snapped down and J.R.'s head fell toward the dashboard. J.R. saved his face from smashing against the dashboard by placing his hand on the dashboard like a football player. It seemed J.R. did not notice the chest belt, although he did fasten the lap belt. After the nose of the plane was now going straight down it then went into a spiral spin. J.R. started getting worried because he learned in the past that it was very difficult to pull out of a spin. The plane kept spinning with the motor off and it was getting closer to the ground and J.R. got more scared than ever. Then suddenly the motor sprung into action and the plane pulled out of the spin. J.R. was considerably relieved but the spin had its consequences. As soon as the plane leveled off J.R. learned that the pilot had been watching him through a rear view mirror. The pilot told J.R. to crank his canopy back to let in some air. It seemed J.R.'s face turned a pale green. J.R. opened the canopy and felt the cold air rushing at his face and felt much better. The pilot then landed the plane and parked it. They both got out and started to walk back to the hangar carrying their parachutes. On the way the pilot related to J.R. his vast experience flying. J.R. said, "Why didn't you tell me this on the way to the plane?" The pilot's face showed a sheepish grin.

About a week later the unit of new gunners were given an introductory flight in a B-17. After the test flight J.R. found this boring. A few days later they were given assignments to become members of a B-24 crew. Everyone was excited with the prospect of finally getting underway. Each B-24 crew consisted of a pilot, co-pilot, navigator, bombardier, radioman, engineer, armorer and three gunners. The B-24 contained six gun locations: the nose turret, the tail turret, the upper turret, the ball turret that was on the bottom and the two waist guns on either side of the plane. Everyone, including the pilot, had to be able to man a gun—usually the waist gun.

The crews were assembled at the flight line for gun and turret assignments. J.R. was very anxious to be assigned to the upper turret. The gunnery officer started by assigning the upper turret to the engineer. The next assignment was the ball turret. The gunner assigned to it was over 6 feet tall. He said, "I can't fit into the turret." The gunnery officer agreed and looked at the crew, looking for the two shortest men. There was one gunner shorter than J.R. and the gunnery officer said you could fit nicely. The gunner said, "I am the tail gunner. I don't want the ball turret." Then the gunnery officer asked who is the armorer. J.R. answered, "I am." The officer said the ball turret is yours. The rest of the positions were very easy to assign. Now that the position of responsibilities was set they were ready to start training.

The very next day they were ordered to attend a briefing. The briefing was about their first flight. Basically it was to be a night flight to give the pilots experience in night flying. This meant the rest of the crew was along for the ride. The take-off was uneventful. When the plane arrived at a cruising altitude, J.R. decided to investigate the ball turret which he was assigned to and which he had no knowledge of. He lowered the ball outside the ship and got inside. It had a very small area and J.R. had to bring his knees up toward his torso. Since it was evening it was pitch black in the turret because there were no lights in the ball. J.R. began to fish for switches when the plane hit an air pocket and dropped suddenly. Being outside the plane and in a strange ball turret he got a good scare. He got out of the turret as quickly as possible and decided not to get into the turret again at night unless it was absolutely necessary.

The next day everyone received orders to report to a specific building for a medical exam. J.R. was called into an examination room where a doctor asked him if he gets cold during the year. J.R. told him no more or less than anyone else. The doctor proceeded to insert two probes consisting of a long thin probe with a lead shield holding radium that was exposed at the end into J.R.'s nostrils. The procedure took two days and was intended to burn out the membrane covering the two back sinuses. When the procedure was completed the doctor informed J.R. that it was done to make sure he could fly in the event he got a cold when flying. But this was not the only physical abuse of young soldiers. One day every airman had to report to the dentist's office to have their wisdom teeth extracted. Fortunately J.R. had no wisdom teeth.

Each barracks had a bulletin board on which flight schedules were posted. Prior to each flight there was a briefing in which all members of the crew had to attend to receive instructions about the flight.

The next flight was during the day and had nonparticipation of the gunners; they were along for the ride. J.R. loved looking out the window while the gunners were seated on the poop deck (an area just above the bomb bay in the rear of the ship). The tall waist gunner advised J.R. he should be seated during the take-off. J.R. paid no attention to the wise advice. After the ship gained sufficient altitude the pilot decided to make a sharp turn. As usual J.R. was standing facing the waist window. When the plane turned the wing dropped, exposing that side of the plane to the ground. Suddenly the waist window J.R. was facing was looking at the ground. That's when gravity took over and J.R. was suddenly propelled toward the open waist window. He flew across the width of the plane and as he got to the open window he knew he had to do something or he would certainly go out the window. J.R. grabbed the edge of the window that slowed his movement toward the open window; and as that happened, the wing of the plane came up and the danger was over. This taught J.R. a lesson. From then on J.R. kept away from the waist window.

The next flight was a gunnery mission. All the gunners were to get experience firing from their positions. This was J.R.'s first experience firing his two .50-caliber machine guns in the ball turret. The plane flew out to the Atlantic Ocean. When it was out far enough the pilot brought the plane down close to the water. They were probably about fifty feet from the water. Then the engineer threw a smoke bomb out the waist window. The idea was to shoot at the bomb that floated on the ocean emitting smoke. On the first pass all the gunners blasted away at the smoke bomb including J.R. As they passed the bomb suddenly there was no more bomb. It was hit and sunk. The pilot instructed J.R. to stop shooting at the smoke bomb. J.R. asked the pilot what he was to shoot at. The pilot told him to shoot at the waves. Since J.R. had to get rid of most of his ammunition in order to get credit for the mission, he promptly let go a volley as the plane prepared to fly past another smoke bomb (the last).

Suddenly the pilot yelled another order at J.R. to ceasefire and explained that there was a fishing traveler passing through a restricted zone used by the bombers for practice. J.R. ceased firing, cleared his guns and brought them up and got out of his turret, satisfied that he did a great job! When the plane landed the gunners removed their guns to be returned to the armory. J.R. placed one gun on each shoulder and walked from the plane to the armory which was a distance of about three blocks away. Before turning in the guns they had to be cleaned properly. The armory had a large table where the guns were cleaned. The bombardier came over to J.R. and asked him to clean his gun. J.R. agreed and asked the pilot and co-pilot if they would like him to clean their guns. They refused the offer.

That night J.R. missed the radio he used to listen to music played by local stations at home and in Quady, Maine. He decided to build a basic crystal radio. The next day there was no flights scheduled. J.R. decided to go to town and obtain some copper wire and a crystal. The idea was to use the earphones built into his leather head gear. J.R. went to the local hardware store and got the copper wire but they did not have a crystal. They recommended the drug store and sure enough the drug store had it. When J.R. returned he put together his idea and tested it by using the end of the copper wire scratching the crystal until he picked up a local station. Then when J.R. went to bed that night he put on his helmet and was lulled to sleep with the music from a local station. In the morning J.R. found the helmet on the floor beside his bed. He was entertained every evening from then on during his training.

The next day the weather became overcast and rainy.

All the flights were cancelled. J.R. learned that the bad weather would hold for two or three more days. J.R. decided it was a great chance to go home in spite of having only a Class A pass that restricted him to a fifty-mile radius off the base. J.R. boarded a train that traveled from Springfield, Mass. to New York. During the trip the train stopped. The passengers were told a hurricane destroyed the tracks ahead and that they would have to be bussed around the area. They boarded the bus and as they passed the area where the tracks were washed out J.R. saw a sight that was astounding. He saw an area several hundred feet wide running from the ocean to the road as if it were plowed by a bulldozer. Sitting in the middle was a large boat lying on its side at least four or five blocks from the ocean. It was an unforgettable sight. The bus skirted the devastated area and returned the passengers to another train on the other side. When J.R. returned home he was greeted royally. He spent some quality time at home and with his girlfriend. On the second day when J.R. was on his way with his girlfriend to take in the delights of the Big Apple to see a show and dine at Tufineties, a famous ice cream parlor on Broadway, J.R. spotted a M.P. stopping servicemen to check their passes. Many servicemen went AWOL (Unauthorized Leave of Absence). J.R. very quickly ducked down a side street to avoid the M.P.s. In the afternoon of the next day J.R. left to return to Westover Air Force Base.

The next mission was a bombing mission. Practice bombs were loaded aboard the plane. The bombs were without the main charge and only had the charge that ignited the main charge. The crew entered the plane and took their usual positions before take-off. When the plane took off and reached the approach to the target J.R. was instructed to remove the carter pins (to arm the bomb) from the bombs. J.R. had to go into the bomb bay walking on a beam about four or five inches wide and start to remove the carter pins that were very large, without pliers. J.R. had all but four pins out when the bomb bay door opened. A violent wind hit him and there was nothing to hold on to. The first thing he did was to grab his hat. Then he turned and ran between the beams that hold up the bombs. When they realized J.R. was in the bomb bay they closed the doors and told J.R. to get out and forget about the last bomb. After he left J.R. remained in the rear area of the plane until the bombs were dropped. Shortly thereafter he was told that there was a bomb that was hanging loosely in the bomb bay. (It didn't drop.) J.R. was asked to try to release it. Without tools it was virtually impossible. J.R. however decided to try. He entered the bomb bay with the door open and the wind blowing and proceeded to the hanging bomb. Without tools the job was all but impossible. J.R. had to try.

The bomb was in a location that was hard to get at. He decided to try to trip the release mechanism on the bomb rack. In order to do it he grabbed onto a beam with one arm, leaned over the side and reached over and pounded the release mechanism with his fist. The rack didn't release, it was frozen. When the pilot saw J.R. hanging over the open bomb bay door he screamed, "Forget it, get the hell out of there." Consequently they rode the bomb down without incident but the crew was sweating it all the way. Incidents such as these and worse happened, and some were not as lucky.

A few days later J.R. heard that one of the planes with a crew that lived in his barracks crashed. Details, as usual, were not available. J.R., however, heard that the bombardier's leg was pinned under the beam of the plane and that one of the maintenance mechanics had to cut the beam with a torch to get him out. This feat was done with fuel on the ground all around the area.

Sometime later in the week the radioman from the ill-fated plane came back from the hospital. He told J.R. that he was a nervous wreck and that he wanted to get out of the Army. About a week or so later another member of the crew of the plane crash came out of the hospital. When he arrived in the barracks J.R. asked him how he felt. He told J.R. that he was in constant pain. J.R. told him to get his ass back to the hospital and to tell them about the pain. A few days later J.R. visited him in the hospital and found him in traction. When they finally released him from the hospital he was free of pain.

One day the FBI descended upon Westover Army Air Force Base. The rumor was that one of the airman wrote home to mom who contacted her senator who called the FBI. This happened because of all of the accidents and plane crashes.

The next mission was a daylight bombing mission—only this time the bombing was with a camera. After the briefing on the way to the plane J.R. had to pick up a camera. The camera turned out to be incredibly large and very heavy. It took J.R. all his strength to carry it the distance to the plane. Then J.R. had to install the large camera that was about three feet wide and two feet deep and weighed about fifty or sixty pounds. When they got airborne the camera had a level on top and J.R. had to adjust the camera if the level indicated the need. They flew the plane up the east coast over all the factories and the idea was for the bombardier to go through his routine and when he pressed the bomb release the picture was taken showing where the bomb would hit. When the film was processed it seemed they only had one direct hit. The rest were not even near misses.

Each flight was designed to give one or more of the crew experience. Toward the end of the training, combat experienced pilots and gunners came aboard to check the pilot and each of the crew. They were now getting close to the conclusion of the training and time to go into combat. There were however a few more training missions left.

Suddenly there was a special briefing called. At the briefing they were told that one of the planes was missing and presumed down. The training commander decided to use a search pattern to try to locate the plane. J.R.'s plane was given their search pattern that was very close to or possibly over the location where the plane went down. When their plane arrived in the pattern area that was over the Adirondack Mountains they had to fly high enough to clear the mountains that were also over the cloud cover that blanketed and lay on top of the mountains. The layer of clouds was so thick they could not see the mountain below. After completing their pattern they returned to their base without any results. After a few days passed they heard that the plane was found with only one survivor, the armorer gunner.

The next day at the briefing for the next mission they were told they were flying a high altitude gun camera mission. This meant they would fly in formation at 32,000 feet with fighter planes attacking the formation. This was a mission to test the gunners. Cameras were attached to the guns and when the gunners pressed their triggers the cameras would record their accuracy.

After the briefing all the gunners picked up their guns and carried them to the plane. J.R. knew he wouldn't be able to get into the turret wearing his teddy bear suit to guard him from the extreme cold at high altitudes and so he picked up and put on a heated suit that looked like a long woolen underwear with electric wires throughout. He put on his flight suit over the heated shirt. When the plane took off and gained altitude and joined up with the other bombers J.R. opened up the hydraulic valve to lower his ball turret outside the bottom of the plane. He then got in the ball turret and started the routine procedure of putting on his helmet and hooking up his intercom, a device consisting of elastic with two discs which fit around the neck on either side of the Adam's apple. The electric cords were plugged in and the oxygen mask was checked. J.R., however, did not check his heated suit. When they finally were in formation the pilot asked each station to report and one by one each position when asked responded.

After a short wait one of the gunners shouted, "Two o'clock high." J.R. swung his turret around, pointing his guns at the approaching fighter plane. J.R. looked at his aiming device that was a brand new and unique invention. It was a small black box mounted on top of the gun mount with what looked like a plain piece of glass mounted at an angle with a circle of light and a dot in the middle. J.R. lined up the fighter plane in his gun sight and found he was out of range of his guns since the wings projected outside the circle. But in a fraction of a second the fighter plane was in range and J.R. pressed his trigger and followed the fighter plane holding him in his gun sight. In less than two seconds the plane was gone.

All this time J.R. was feeling very cold. He kept reaching below his seat for the thermostat that he kept adjusting. When another fighter plane was about to attack and he had to press the trigger he found he couldn't press the trigger and that was when he realized he was in trouble; the heated suit was not working. J.R. quickly called the pilot and explained his problem. The pilot (they called him the old man) told J.R. to come forward to the pilot's compartment which was heated.

This was no easy task, especially since J.R. was in the ball turret. He had to detach all his electrical connections and oxygen connection and attach an oxygen bottle called the walk around bottle. He then had to place the turret in the landing position and open the hatch door so he could exit the turret. J.R. then had to make his way through the bomb bay to get to the front of the ship. When he arrived he first realized he was in serious trouble. The oxygen bottle had a pressure indicator that read empty. He had to act quickly or he would be dead in a minute or less. On the floor in back of the pilot's compartment sat the co-pilot. It seemed the pilot was being checked out by an experienced pilot who took the co-pilot's seat. J.R. shouted over the roar of the engines, explaining his problem. The co-pilot without hesitation immediately detached his oxygen connection and gave it to J.R. who connected the oxygen to his mask, took a few breaths and then connected the oxygen to the walk around bottle until the gauge read full. J.R. then handed the oxygen tube back to the co-pilot who ordered J.R. to go back to the rear. When J.R. arrived in the rear a gunnery instructor who was working with the gunners immediately took off his heavy jacket and made J.R. put his arm into the sleeves, putting on the jacket backwards. The instructor sat J.R. down to await their landing.

J.R. felt disoriented and poorly. When the plane landed and taxied to a stop, there was a jeep awaiting J.R. He climbed out of the plane and into the jeep that took him to the base hospital. J.R. was escorted into the hospital and seated awaiting the doctor. After a short wait two doctors entered the room. One doctor seemed to be instructing the other. J.R. got up, leaning against a desk. He reached out his hands upon the doctor's request. While the doctor was trying to teach his intern J.R. started to slip down the side of the desk he was leaning against. The doctor noticed and grabbed J.R. before he fell to the ground. The doctor yelled for an orderly to bring a wheelchair. At this point J.R. started to slowly lose consciousness. His hearing and vision started to fade until he totally lost consciousness. Sometime later when he regained consciousness he was in bed in a private room with the covers up to his neck. His entire crew led by the pilot started to enter the room and J.R. seeing them broke down and cried.. The pilot quickly herded the crew out of the room. J.R.'s reaction was caused by the fact that he let his buddies down and that he lost his last chance to get overseas and contribute in a meaningful way to the war effort.

The next day J.R. realized he hadn't written home for some time and his mother would be concerned since he was flying. He sent word and asked one of his buddies to visit him. When he arrived J.R. asked him to write home for him since his hands were bandaged holding ice cubes. J.R. dictated the letter explaining that he was injured and was in the base hospital but it was nothing serious. Of course at this point J.R. did not know if he would lose his fingers or hands. The head surgeon came in every day to see if gangrene set in. It was a waiting game. One day J.R. noticed his thumb had developed a natural cast as hard as stone. When the chief surgeon came in one day with the ward doctor he told the ward doctor to remove the ugly cast. When the surgeon left the ward the doctor told J.R. he will peel off the cast little by little. Each day he peeled off a little more. By the end of the week the ward doctor had the cast about three quarters of the way off. Shortly thereafter the surgeon showed up and when he saw the remainder of the cast still on he made a few nasty remarks about the ward doctor. He then placed his fingernail under the cast and, getting a firm grasp, pulled the cast off along with J.R.'s fingernail. J.R. just collapsed to the floor and the surgeon made no effort to catch him.

During his stay in the hospital an announcement was made that Groucho Marx was coming to the hospital to entertain. On the day of Groucho's arrival everyone was assembled in an auditorium. When J.R. entered he spotted a friend laying on a gurney. He was the survivor of the plane crash J.R. and his crew were searching for. J.R. greeted him warmly. His friend started the conversation by explaining that the surgeon cut off one hand and that he was waiting for them to cut off the other hand. His explanation was done in a very jovial manner. In fact their entire conversation was laced with jokes. When the lights were lowered as a signal to be seated J.R. said so long and good luck. Before the entertainment began J.R. could not understand his friend's attitude. How can you kid about your hands and feet being cut off? The reason for the amputation was frostbite. Since J.R. was in the hospital for the same thing not a word was said about the ordeal. Much later J.R. came to understand his friend's attitude. His friend had been sleeping on the poop deck that was over the bomb bay when the plane came down out of the clouds to try to determine where they were. Unfortunately the clouds were laying on the mountains, so the plane crashed. When his friend gained consciousness after the crash he found his shipmates were a horrible sight. His immediate thought was to get the hell out of there. Without thinking he jumped out of the waist window onto the snowy mountain where he stayed for two days and two nights. The temperature there was around thirty-two degrees below zero. He was located when the residents living near the mountain saw flares that the plane fired off before they crashed. Then they heard the crash and notified the authorities. Search parties were sent up the side of the mountain where they found J.R.'s friend.

A few days later J.R. noticed orderlies carrying two pilots on stretchers into the ward across the hall. They were obviously involved in a plane crash. Their heads were swollen to almost double their normal size. It was a terrible sight. A short time later J.R. was released from the hospital. He was told he would have to wait for reassignment. While waiting one day J.R. was standing on the platform at the entrance to the barracks when a column of German prisoners of war came marching by. When suddenly a very young German prisoner speaking in German started cursing J.R. as a dirty rotten Jew. J.R. stared at him saying nothing as he marched by.

A few days later J.R. was assigned to a new crew. Once again J.R. was flying training missions. On the second mission two gunners came to him for help. It seemed the tail gunner was stuck in his turret. The door refused to open. Although J.R. was not taught anything about any turret he went along to the tail. When he saw the doors on the tail turret resembled the door on the New York City subway trains he knew just what he had to do to get the tail gunner out of the turret. J.R. placed his hands between the two doors and with all his might he sprung the doors open.

The next mission was a long distance flight from Westover Army Air Force Base in Massachusetts to Cape Hatterus and back. This was to give the pilot, co-pilot, navigator and radioman experience in long distance flight. The flight to Cape Hatterus was uneventful as was the flight back until the radioman, "Chinnery," called the navigator and asked him if they could be off course since he was receiving a very strong signal from Boston. The navigator said, no, we should be arriving back at Westover shortly.

However that was not to be. It seemed shortly thereafter they were flying along the coast of Maine. The pilot then turned the plane around and started back down the coast. At this point the pilot decided to call in for help. For some reason the pilot was told to go due east which took him out toward England. When the plane was out in the ocean far enough and the radioman could not raise anyone and the gas gauge read empty, the pilot turned around and headed west toward land.

About this time the engineer went around trying to get rid of the sandwiches he had left. He came over to J.R. and asked if he wanted a sandwich; no one felt like eating. J.R. asked him what he had. J.R. took one of the sandwiches and ate it. Then the navigator asked J.R. to look out of the forward window and see if he could see land and if he did to let him know. J.R. concentrated on his task until he heard some movement behind him. He turned around and saw the navigator crawling through the entrance to the navigator compartment carrying his parachute in order to exit the area. J.R. was annoyed at not being told to leave the compartment. He grabbed his parachute and rushed after him.

At this point the forward compartment of the plane was crowded. The pilot was trying to alert everyone to be prepared for a signal to bail out, but he couldn't get a response from the men in the rear area. He then ordered the officer who came along for the ride to go to the rear and alert them. But the officer, obviously scared stiff, did not budge. Then the pilot asked J.R. to wake up the men in the rear compartment, but the officer blocked the way. J.R., not wanting to push the officer out of the way, decided to go around.

The route around lay between the center beam and the curved body of the plane with the bomb bay door below.

Holding his parachute in one hand and holding one of the beams J.R. stepped on the curved body of the plane and swung around the beam and finally finding the bottom beam that he used to get to the rear. When he got there the door to the rear area was closed. He opened the door and there were four men fast asleep. He woke the second officer who was along for the ride and told him to tell the rest of them to prepare to bail out. The response was "What?" J.R. told him he wasn't going to enter the rear, and insisted he would sit in the doorway. He told them when the bomb bay door opened and the horn blew it was their signal to bail out—"And if I don't jump, push me!"

In the meantime J.R. sat at the entrance to the rear compartment and looked at the ocean streaking by through a crack in the bomb bay door. Then suddenly J.R. saw land and knew they made it. At this point the pilot called the tower of the landing field they were approaching. The landing field was closed at this time but always had someone on duty in the tower. The controller on duty at the time answered. The pilot explained to him he was coming in for an emergency landing and he told him to turn on the landing lights. The pilot explained he was low on fuel and would not circle and would come in low and to prepare to refuel his plane.

The landing was smooth. As soon as the plane touched down and slowed the pilot pulled the plane off the landing strip and parked the plane and raced the engine before cutting them off. The pilot opened the bomb bay so the crew could exit the plane but J.R. and the engineer decided to check the gas tanks. They climbed out onto the wing and opened the gas cap and with a flashlight they looked into the tank and saw the bottom of the tanks. There was no fuel in the tanks. It was 3 a.m. and all of the crew was taken to an empty barracks where they could stay until dawn. During their stay the pilot revealed how he was able to fly the plane with so little fuel. He realized that in order for him to make land he would have to reduce the use of fuel. He did this by lowering the fuel setting of the controls. This of course meant that he couldn't maintain his altitude. However, he knew he had to come down until he reached the airport.

When the crew entered the empty barracks the only place to sit down and relax was the floor. They had three or four hours to kill. By dawn the plane was fueled and the crew boarded for the flight back to Westover. J.R. was told later on that his plane had a history of getting lost.

At this point the war was nearing an end. J.R. learned that the crew he trained with and lost when he was injured and in the hospital had an easy time in combat. They flew out of England and their mission was to bomb Berlin. They had no fighter plane opposition and very little flack.

Before the next mission J.R. flew he was told he would no longer be the ball gunner. His new position was the nose turret. It seemed bombing tactics caused changes. Instead of the bombardier using his bomb sight to hit a target they decided to use pattern bombing. This eliminated the bombardier; instead the armorer gunner in the nose turret pulled the switch to drop the bombs. Of course, the lead bomber in a group composed of 100 bombers had a bombardier and when he opened the bomb doors all the rest of the bombers opened theirs; and when the lead bomber dropped his bombs the rest of the bombers dropped theirs.

The next mission did not involve the gunners but they were all required to man their turrets. J.R. entered the nose turret and after an hour or so was sorry he did not take his heavy mittens. The turret was very cold partly because it was in the front of the plane and the air penetrated. J.R.'s hands which were previously frozen became very painful. He called the pilot and asked permission to leave the turret. The pilot refused to allow him to leave. J.R. took a great dislike for the pilot and decided to return to the hospital and inform them of his problem or ask for a transfer out of the bomber. But before J.R. could do anything providence changed everything. The war in Europe was over. Germany surrendered. That was the last J.R. flew in a B-24 Liberator. Since the war in the Pacific was still raging the Air Corps needed crews for the B-29s. Since the B-29 was considerably different than the B-24 it was necessary to go to a different gunnery school than after the school to B-29 transitional training.

J.R. soon received orders to go from Westover, Mass. to Fort Myers, Florida. The living conditions were good compared to those in Texas where they lived in a barrack that was a former chicken coop. While waiting for the start of changes a few of the fellows decided to take a sunbath on the lawn outside the barracks. They took mattresses and stretched out on the lawn in the buff. It seemed across the roadway was a barracks that was occupied by WACs. One of the men had a pet duck that he brought out with him and allowed the duck to run free. It was a mistake. Before he could do anything the duck took off across the roadway with his owner after him in the buff! Everyone yelled after him but he kept after the duck until he caught the duck. And with the duck firmly in his grasp he promptly walked back to the barracks. When J.R. decided to sun himself he lay on his mattress for about fifteen minutes and very quickly got up and ran inside the barracks with his mattress. J.R. thought the rest of the guys were crazy, the sun was too strong for him.

In no time at all they were ordered to start gunnery school. Just as before he was shooting shotguns, the only difference was when they flew in a B-24 that was equipped with remote controlled turrets instead of the usual turrets on the B-24. The B-29 had remote controlled turrets with the controller at the waist window. One day a select few along with J.R. went for a flight and J.R. was selected to fire the remote control guns. The plane flew along the coast and there was a thin strip of land off the coast where they placed about a half a dozen large targets. J.R. checked his gun sight and fired away. He could see the tracer bullets hitting the targets as the plane passed them. He was delighted because with this system he did not get the heavy vibration he got in the ball turret.

But before J.R. completed the gunnery school, the war with Japan was over.

VIII
Flying B-24s Ends

Now it was just a matter of time before J.R. received his freedom. The Army Air Force decided at that time to bring the airmen overseas home first (a logical step). In order to do this they had to make plans to replace them with new recruits. In order to service the new recruits they shipped J.R. from Fort Myers, Florida to Las Vegas, Nevada, once again by troop train. After getting settled in one of the barracks J.R. along with a number of others were assigned to work in one of the warehouses where G.I. clothing was stored. On the inside it had a long counter and an area behind the counter for personnel who handed out the clothing. Behind the personnel were small cubicles about eight feet high holding the clothing to be given to the recruits. Each of the men who were assigned to work there were positioned along the counter with the clothing they were to hand out located in bins behind them. J.R. was assigned shirts. He asked each of them, "What size shirt?" Most knew but some didn't, so J.R. said, "You look like a 15-1/2–32. If it's wrong, come back and exchange it."

The next day when J.R. came to the warehouse to work he noticed a few men gathered around a box taking out leather jackets. These jackets were supposed to be given to pilots but were misdirected. The jackets quickly disappeared. During the day a captain appeared and explained to all the men working in the warehouse that there had been an unusually large shrinkage of inventory and anyone caught with stolen contraband will be punished severely. The next day the barracks was raided and searched. Nothing was found. After the search J.R. was told that one fellow got a footlocker and stuffed it with clothing he took and mailed it home.

One day a Warrant Officer came in and asked if there was anyone who had training in accounting. J.R. having had successful experience in volunteering said he had accounting experience, he took the subject up at NYU. The officer explained he needed a crew of men to pick up all the guns, ammunition and equipment the Air Force had at this base and return them to Army Ordnance. J.R. was placed in charge of the crew of men and given a truck and a civilian secretary. In the military this was G.I. heaven. In addition to the above J.R. was exempt from all of the activities required of the other members of the corps which included close order drill and marching imposed to keep the men busy while they waited for release from service.

J.R. was seated in front of the truck with the driver, with his men in back. They went out to the firing ranges to pick up the .50-caliber machine guns and ammunition. They then went to Army Ordnance where his crew unloaded the truck. When they returned J.R. instructed his secretary how to record the equipment returned to Army Ordnance. The most peculiar part of this whole event is that the officer that selected them never returned. They never saw him again.

The next day orders were issued that all men, officers and enlisted men were to wear official dress (O.D.s) when eating supper.

J.R. decided to quit work a little early instead of working up to supper and then go to supper in their work clothes since it was mandatory to wear dress clothes for supper. While J.R. and a friend were in the barracks an officer entered and asked them why they weren't outside for close order drill. J.R. explained that he was presently assigned to special duty relieving him from all other duties and that he was in the barracks in order to change into O.D.s for supper. The officer (a shave tail—slang for thirty-day wonder) ordered them to report out front for close order drill and left very quickly.

Since J.R. had close to three and a half years of service and about one year of flying time and was very close to being released from service he wasn't going to be doing close order drill. Especially after being ordered by a thirty-day wonder (a brand new second lieutenant).

J.R. looked at his friend and asked, "Are you going out for close order drill?" His friend said no. J.R. said, "Let's get the hell out of here." J.R. quickly headed for the rear exit with his friend close behind.

After all the equipment was returned to ordinance the job was complete. Since the officer who originated J.R.'s group mission never returned and he had no orders of any further operations, J.R. decided to get some rest and relaxation. Hearing about an Army rest camp in the mountains a relatively short distance outside of Las Vegas, he decided to take the entire crew first to a luxurious skiing lodge near the rest camp. They arrived at the lodge early that morning. When they entered the lodge they walked into a room with a bar on one side and line of slot machines on the other side. Beyond these areas was a dining room. As soon as the group entered the room they went directly to the slot machines. J.R. and his secretary took a seat at the bar. They were at the bar for quite a while talking to the bartender when J.R. became bored and went over to the men playing the slot machines. None of the men won anything. J.R.

asked if anyone was tired of losing their money. One of the men said, "You can have my machine." J.R. got a handful of quarters from the bartender and started to play. The third quarter hit the jackpot. The quarters started to fall into the tray; when the tray was full they started to bounce onto the floor. The fellow that gave up the machine went ballistic but soon realized J.R. was giving him this vacation instead of doing close order drill. The other fellows chimed in and insisted that J.R. pay for breakfast. He readily agreed without knowing what it would cost him. With both his pockets jammed full of quarters they moved into the dining room and sat down at a large table. No one took a full breakfast. They all ordered a cup of coffee and a muffin or toast. When J.R. got the bill he could hardly believe it. The bill was more than J.R. won in quarters. They finally left to return to the rest camp for lunch. Since it was Christmas the menu was turkey with all the trimmings. J.R. was offered a turkey leg and was told he could have seconds if he wished. What a wonderful meal, the best he could remember having since he was in the service. In the afternoon they all returned to camp.

Later that week J.R. returned to the rest camp but at the time he had no transportation. He decided to hitchhike a ride. After trying for a short while he got a ride on the back of a pick-up truck. The ride was pleasant in the first half but as they climbed the mountain it became colder and colder, especially since J.R. was wearing his summer uniform. That evening since it was Christmas all the servicemen at the rest camp were invited to the skiing lodge. There was dancing going on but since J.R. didn't have a partner to dance with he sat at the bar where he received free drinks. He sat there all evening until he was as drunk as can be. When it was time to return to the rest camp all the servicemen were drunk since drinks were on the house. It seemed the rest camp sent a truck along with several to help get all the men back to camp safely. The truck was parked about twelve or fifteen feet from the entrance and when the men came out of the lodge, each one would slip and fall. The truck driver and his assistant grabbed each one and assisted them and tossed them into the truck. J.R. didn't remember the trip back to camp or being put to bed! The first thing he remembered the next day was a sergeant inviting everyone to lunch since they all slept through breakfast. When J.R. woke up he felt terrible, the room was spinning around. He had a terrible hangover. Although he knew they had a wonderful lunch prepared he just couldn't make it.

When New Year's Day arrived J.R. was still waiting to be released into civilian life. He had nothing to do. He decided to visit one of the casinos in Las Vegas. When J.R. arrived in town he wandered from casino to casino looking at the slot machines, the crap games and card games. In one of the casinos he saw a crowd around one of the crap tables. It seemed a high roller came in and was betting thousands of dollars that made the game exciting for everyone. J.R. also noticed they were giving the gambler free drinks. At each casino J.R. visited he asked the dealers for a pair of discarded dice for a memento. He collected a pair of dice from every casino. That evening while J.R. was wandering around one of the casinos he came upon a bingo game. He noticed that each game cost twenty-five cents and if you won you could receive from $10 to $25. Since J.R. had only a few dollars he felt bingo would provide him some entertainment for the rest of the evening or at least until his money ran out. Game after game went by and J.R. won nothing. In fact, the entire time he was playing up to the final game he won nothing. Finally they announced the last game and the winner would receive $100. The game went on for some time as the caller yelled out each number. Finally J.R. yelled out “Bingo!” Well, what a commotion. Of course mostly women were playing. One of the women yelled out, “Look, a soldier won.” When J.R. went to the cashier he received the $100 in silver dollars. As he received them he kept putting them into different pockets and with his clothing weighing him down he decided to go back to the camp. As he was leaving he passed the $1 slot machines. J.R. felt since he had so many silver dollars he could afford to try a few dollars. But the effort was in vain so he gave up and returned to camp.

It wasn’t too long thereafter that he received his orders to report to Fort Dix for discharge. His orders read that he was to travel from Las Vegas to New York by troop train. The train was to leave that afternoon. J.R. was approached by one of the fellows in the outfit who asked him if he would like to hitch a flight home. Since J.R. hated troop trains he thought it was a good idea. They went to the flight line and asked about flights going east. The only flight at all was a flight going to Los Angeles. J.R.’s friend said they will take it and get a flight east in Los Angeles. About two hours later a flight going east landed. The flight was going to El Paso, Texas. The plane refueled and was ready to leave. It seemed the plane was a DC-3, the workhorse of the Air Force. It had no seats, it was a cargo plane. The flight was a short one over a mountain range. They landed at a large Air Force Base with a lot of flight activity. Planes were flying in and out. Upon arrival they were directed to a large hangar where there were over a hundred chairs lined up in rows with almost as many soldiers awaiting transportation. Upon arrival everyone seeking a flight signed in with the sergeant in charge and as the planes were available the names of those who signed in were called. When J.R. and his friend signed in the sergeant told them that they couldn't obtain a flight until tomorrow. They were informed they could get supper and breakfast in the mess hall and a bunk for the night. It was a very large Air Force Base with a lot of friendly people running it.

The next morning J.R. and his friend reported to the sergeant in charge and asked him how much longer they would have to wait. It seemed there was a lot of aircraft activity at this base. Planes from all the services landed at this base both day and night. The sergeant told them they were at the top of the list and they would be called shortly. It seemed a large plane seating over a dozen people came in and was leaving after being refueled. In the meantime the sergeant started to call out a long list of names. The last name called was J.R.'s friend. The flight was going to Miami. This annoyed J.R. considerably. But he realized he would be the first to be called for the next flight. All those who were called left for their flight while J.R. waited. It wasn't long before J.R.'s name was called. He was told it was a Navy plane and a two-seater. J.R. was the only passenger. The Navy plane was headed for Jacksonville, Florida. Carrying his luggage and his parachute J.R. walked out to the flight line. He was directed to the plane which was an aircraft carrier training plane. He met the pilot and they both climbed aboard. J.R. had to climb onto the wing and then climb into the rear seat. The pilot started up the engine and taxied the plane onto the runway. J.R. strapped himself in and the plane roared down the runway. To J.R. it felt like being in a golf cart. He was used to a B-24. The plane lifted off the runway and quickly rose to about five or six thousand feet. The view was spectacular. J.R. had a small address book that contained a detailed map of the

U.S. He could see every detail on the ground—all the roads, cars and people.

He followed the progress of the plane on his map. About halfway to Jacksonville they landed at a small naval station on the Gulf coast to refuel. J.R. did not know the pilot wanted to land in order to refuel. Over the intercom he asked the pilot if there was any problem. This was when the pilot started to descend. The pilot was furious since his air to ground radio was open at the time. When the refueling was completed and the pilot was prepared to leave he got into the plane and asked J.R. to help him lock the wing into position. Since the plane was a carrier plane the wing folded up and when the pilot attempted to bring the wing down sometimes it didn't lock into place. To insure it locked into place J.R. had to press the end of the wing hard. In short order they were back in the air on their way to Jacksonville. On route they flew over Pensacola, Florida where there was a large Navy base. J.R. noticed an aircraft carrier that looked like a postage stamp. How does a plane land on a postage stamp? Very shortly thereafter they approached a Naval Air Station in Jacksonville, Florida that had three Navy bases. J.R. was told he could get a flight to New York in a Naval Air Base located on the other side of Jacksonville. The pilot and J.R., carrying their flight bag and parachute, proceeded to take a long walk through Jacksonville. When they arrived at the Air Base they were told that MATS (Military Air Transport Service) had a scheduled service along the East Coast out of the base. J.R. signed up for a flight to New York City. Since MATS was run exactly like all the airlines in the U.S. J.R. had to turn in his parachute. After flying with a parachute for so long it was a very unsettling feeling flying without one.

Since the flight didn't leave for an hour or so J.R. decided to take a short walk and visit the mess hall. Throughout his military career J.R. had difficulties with the food but the Navy food at this base was the worst he experienced. J.R. walked out of the mess hall and ate nothing. Upon leaving the mess hall J.R. was approached by an S.P. who told him he was wearing his hat wrong. J.R. asked him what he knew about an Air Force uniform, then he showed him his marks on his sleeve explaining that it represented three years of service. He told the S.P. he was a guest and that he was on his way to Fort Dix for release from the service. With that J.R. walked away. Shortly after J.R. arrived at the base terminal. A list of names were called and J.R.'s name was called third from last. They then proceeded to board a large four-engine transport plane. In a short while the engines started up and the plane taxied out to the flight strip and it took off.

When they reached Washington, D.C. the plane circled an airport and landed. J.R. and the last two passengers on the flight were told that the plane had mechanical problems and therefore had to land and that the substitute plane carried less passengers. J.R. asked if they could get another plane to New York and was told none were scheduled. J.R. decided since he was so close to N.Y. he would take the train. The other two who lost their transportation to N.Y. joined J.R. They made their way to the entrance of the base where the (S.P.) Sea Police, who guarded the gate, refused to allow them to leave. J.R. insisted on speaking to the officer in charge. The S.P. agreed and called and requested a supervisor to make his way to the gate. In the meantime, as the group stood waiting a car approached the gate and stopped. An officer saw the group was standing near the gate and realized they were being denied exit. He asked the S.P. what was the problem. The S.P. responded explaining that they had no exit pass. The officer asked J.R. where he was going. J.R. explained. The officer told them to hop into the car, he would be glad to take them to the station and told the S.P. he would take the responsibility. The S.P. said OK and the group departed.

Upon arrival at the train station J.R. promptly purchased a ticket and was directed to the platform where the train for New York was waiting to receive passengers. There was a large wrought iron fence in the front of all the train platforms. While waiting for the gate to the platform to open J.R. noticed a group of G.I.s entering from another gate and heading for his platform. J.R. recognized one of them as a friend that was in his gunnery school and decided to find him and find out what happened to him. After the group of G.I.s boarded the train J.R.'s gate was opened. Instead of grabbing a seat he raced through the train until he found him. Their conversation was brief since his friend was reluctant to talk of his experience in detail. He did explain that his bomber was shot down over Italy by a German jet on their way to bomb the Polesty oil fields. He was not hurt when he bailed out and found by an Italian partisan who took him to their camp in the mountains. He was treated royally. He was given the best of everything they had. They even gave him a girl to live with him. When the conversation ended J.R. made his way back to the friend he was traveling with. By that time all the seats were taken. J.R. decided to try his luck in the parlor car that was carpeted and had living room chairs, tables, etc., but there were no seats available. There was nothing left to do other than standing the rest of the way or sitting on the carpeted floor. J.R. chose to sit on the floor. The trip was relatively short.

When he arrived in New York J.R. took a subway train home. What a greeting he got at the door! His dog (Stranger), who was at least fifteen years old or older, with a running start jumped and hit him in the stomach, knocking him down. Then he just went wild. He ran down the foyer into the living room jumping onto a chair and back to J.R., jumping on him and licking his face. That evening Gussie, J.R.'s mother, made one of her famous delicious meals which J.R. devoured. The next day he had an upset stomach. J.R. was not used to eating such large meals.

IX
Free at Last

A few days later J.R. reported to Fort Dix in New Jersey for processing out of the service. As usual it was hurry up and wait.

Finally he was called and he went through the process of paperwork and physical exams. Toward the end he was asked if he had any ailments or injuries to report. Although J.R. had his high altitude frostbite and his sinus membrane removed he told them no injuries. At this completion of the processing they gave J.R. a number of medals, the last medal was for sharpshooter with a .45-caliber automatic. J.R. was surprised since no one told him he did well when he fired the weapon over a year ago.

When the process was over and he was released, J.R. was delighted. It felt as if he was being released from prison. When J.R. joined the Air Force he joined to help win the war and work his way up the ranks. Instead he was sent to college or sent to armorer school. One day J.R. decided to end what he felt was the stupidity of the decision-makers. He signed up for cadets. Perhaps if he became a pilot he would break through and achieve his goal. But even that didn't work. Therefore all the years he spent as a private or a corporal he was a prisoner who couldn't leave without being lucky enough to get a pass, and living in a barracks with all the other prisoners. Even if J.R. received a pass the nearest town wasn't worth visiting. In one camp, in order to leave, even if you had a pass an enlisted man had to sing the Air Force song!

After J.R. left the service he was asked a number of times where he served overseas. He explained that he served three-and-a-half years in the States. Everyone he told said he was lucky. But he did not feel that way, especially since his crew had only six missions over Berlin with practically no opposition. J.R. felt he was denied the opportunity of using his ability to contribute to the winning of the war, which left him very bitter concerning the Army Air Corps officers of World War II.